I0510528

THIS BOOK IS DEDICATED TO MY FAMILY, MY FRIENDS AND ALL
MY COLLEAGUES WHOM I LOVED WORKING WITH AND WITH SPE-
CIAL THANKS TO THOSE WHO MADE MY LIFE TOUGH SO THAT I
COULD IMPROVISE

TEJPAL SALUJA

Tejpal Saluja

This book is all about the experiences which a male member of the Indian society has to face and an interesting journey from being a novice to an experienced person in corporate life with special reference to BFSI sector. The book touches theories and application of management rules and practices in real life and covers area like human resource, finance, sales, operations, training and human life experience like success, cheating, laughter, sorrow, failure and also about act of smartness, foolishness and standing even after failure. So, let's start evolution process...

PART A

CHAPTER 1 BEGINNING

At the innocent age of 10 when your class teacher asks in the class" *Come on students! Tell me what do you want to become?"*. And then you wake up from your dream world and see all those studious girls, and few boys too, raising their hands and shouting" *Ma'am, Ma'am, May I?"*. What do you see? *Half of the class wants to be scientist and half of them want to go to Mars!!!* And here I am, *thinking to go in Army or becoming a business man or simple becoming an actor or even Superman!* However, in reality, I say" *Ma'am, I want to become an Astronaut."* See, simple lie simple living. First rule of life whatever your dream be sometimes, it's good to follow herd.

Now I have grown up listening to great love songs of 90's and especially *"Papa kehte hai bada naam karega! Beta hamara aisa kaam karega!"* Of course, you guessed right in your mind. I was believer of next two lines of the song. So, listening to music, watching cartoons and day dreaming and doing other activities came the age of 15. Now till that age some of my scientists and astronauts' friends were either struggling with Physics or Maths or Chemistry and some were like me, struggling with all!

At this stage you see your dear uncle and aunt and all relatives and even parents! becoming too much interested in one single question -"*Beta, aage kya socha hai? Kya banoge?"* Now, neither my parents nor anyone in my family was a politician: so that I could say

"I will become Prime Minster of India." So, like a defeated warrior, I would say *"Jo aap bolo"* And then I came to know that there may be all types of jobs and skills to survive and excel in life but like USA and USSR there were only two super professions – Doctor and Engineer!

Now since my intelligence and PCM were both on parallel tracks, I decided to follow my belief in the power of money and chose the Third front of World – Commerce. Now here through the knowledge and wisdom running in DNA of my family and my uncle, auntie, I came to know about a super magical word like "Shazam-MBA!" Though I had been fascinated about corporate life since I paid a visit to a very plush office of a big Indian Company. Now imagine as a kid aged 12 you are seeing marble staircase, wooden inserts, nice sofas, revolving chairs, false ceiling, blinds on windows, a cheerful receptionist, cool white boxes *(yeah! Yeah! computers of that age looked like that only)* and behind that good happy environment, you would see people dressed in smart formals with their shirts tucked in and every one wearing polished shoes! *Apart from Armed forces, I never saw such cool environment. Not to compare with the office my dad used to work at though he was working in a nationalised bank at very good post.*

So, being MBA will land me here? My childhood fascination?" Yes of course! Who else?" Then I learned another rule of life- not all become great scientist and doctors some become the smart tycoons as well. So, till 18 I dreamed of becoming a corporate person. Worked hard for that. Got into commerce college and also doing professional coaching for my dream work! Till then my few friends had already started going to their father's shop, few had just vanished out of sight, dreams of few becoming Thomas Elva Addison and Neil Armstrong had sunk like Titanic. But few were determined to succeed in their dreams. Don't underestimate me I was one of them.

Now in college I came to know about my capacity to act in urgency and believing in small goals and smart efforts. So, I used to just study a day, sorry night before the graduation exams, be an environment friendly person (used to fill only main sheet, NO SUPPLIMENTARY COPIES!), and believing in descent passing marks. My obsession of very high percentage had some-how left me mid-way of life. Of course, I still had engineer and doctor friends who were all sharing their great experience of college lives (yes! you guessed the right word starting from R and ending with G) their respect to their seniors (though mostly forced). Then there were friends who are going to become good

teachers and some will dream of landing into Airlines and what all. Some changed their status from PCM to commerce. Next rule – life has various options.

Finally, here I am! Completed my graduation and my professional course half way via various attempts and doing re learning for long. Mid way also tried coaching for MBA. I told you about my dream na! Though my experience was quite different. How? I went on hunting with best classes and I took entrance in the best coaching of town. And very enthusiastically, I went for first day of coaching. My eyes fell wide open when I came to see almost 100 students there and that too was first batch! There were total 3 batches in a day. Where those students during my counselling? Had I seen them all, I wouldn't have dared to join at all!

Still regaining consciousness and gathering the left-over confidence I tried to grasp the lectures. Suddenly I met my old friend whom I didn't liked at all" Maths" and this time that idiot was disguised in aptitude, logical reasoning. Next rule – life has a funny way of testing your skills.

Now I came to know logical thinking in a different way. 300 students in one coaching. 5 such coaching's in the town. All of them preparing for CAT. Some were too risk averse. They will give all abbreviated three- or four-letter exams. Number of colleges in the city, near about 10. Seats allotted to each college 60. Not even counting near locations college and colleges in other cities of the state. So, if everyone was going to get into MBA college and earn a degree, how many jobs does any company offers? Decided then only – NO MBA. Next rule – Not every path is a direct path to success.

And in mid-way like other students I too had parties and cute girlfriend, to spend my father's money , and helping friend (who would listen me with interest when I would say *"bhai, usne mujhe dekha"* to a situation one he will console me by saying" *bhai, chod! wo apne type ki nahi hai"*) He will also encourage me when I would fail and we together used to hear a good song by Adnan Sami *"Mujh ko bhi to lift karade"*. To be honest, my family supported me during my study illusion and efforts and helped me by standing besides me. Next rule – Say Thanks to your family and friends.

Now I don't know how many of you landed into job by choice- after all who wants to work for money when in college, life was simple on father's money. I wanted to do job for pleasure and sat- isfaction (I am still searching for that job). Most of us (boys) land in job to show to their Ex *"You left the diamond baby!"* I was not an exception to that extent. Although that was one of the reasons. In this relationship I came to know about one great Indian rule. – If you want to settle in life with a good girl, go get a job where you have PF deduction!

So, after all emotional up's and down- I am ready to say" Dear *World! Here I come in Job world"*

CHAPTER 2 – JOB HUNT

Now after having decided to get into job, which was after my failed attempt in going for business twice. Though that helped me in knowing one thing, for success you need to believe in yourself. Now in India if your dad is a known member of society, getting a part time job to learn experience is like asking for a pen from a boy in exam. All you will get is........you know that. People will make such a face and say" *Are tum to unke.... bete ho na? Aisa job karoge? Log kua kahenge?*" So, if you are living in a metro city then good, else look for work in another city. And by this time your favourite newspaper section is REQUIREMENTS. And your new favourite work in a cybercafé is uploading CV on job portals and applying for jobs (earlier it used to be chat messengers, remember the old days!) Even paying visits to job consultants. All that day long hunting and surviving on a *baked samosa or vada pav or bhel.*

Hence, I decided to look for job in another city. It was a travelling time of first 90 min and then reduced to 60 min and now to 45 min. All thanks to good roads! I used to use public transport. Got me a chance to see and learn from many persons by observing. Next rule – You can learn anywhere and from anywhere. I learned the importance of equation of distance and time. So, if you catch a bus or train at 08.00 AM that we will have a different impact on distance than you catching a bus or train at 08.15 or say 08.30 AM. Also learned that I can stand in the 1'ft area at least for an hour or so and even while returning to home. Had I been in old times then I would have made Great Gods come to me a and say" *Bachcha, hum tumahri tapasya se prassan hue! Mango ky mangte ho?"*

And as if this was not enough. Recall the situation- you were used to wear jeans and T- shirts with all funky and rebel quotes. Hairstyle like a movie star. And going to Gym to make your lean body look macho. Now suddenly you have to buy or I should say get stitched at least one or two trouser and you buy two formal shirts. Now with your copies of certificates and resume copies too (after all I too was risk adverse person, so applied for all jobs) and your well ironed dress and polished shoes, you catch a bus/ train and some idiot trips on you in crowd! And then you get off the bus/train and that feeling like a commando who has passed after 30 days survival training.

After all the hardships you somehow get an interview call. The night before, you become a great disciple of God and that continues till you get the desired result. Though in between, I switched my devotion to various Gods according to the days of interview. Anyways reaching the place of interview after contributing in GDP via getting shoe polished and also accumulating blessings from few whom I would give some alms, I would face all type of questions. Some very routine like" *Tell us about yourself"* As if they suppose that I am a holy saint who has realised the true potential of inner self. Some other were like" Tell us about your family". Now the situation is – if I tell them that I am from a good affluent family then they will say *"then why do you need the job"?* And if I tell them that I am from a poor family then they will say" *will you work overtime?"* Some questions were too stupid" *Why do you need this job?".* I wanted to yell" *To show my family and my neighbours, my entire society, my all relatives and my Ex- that I am not useless."* Instead I would say *"To prove my skills and be an asset to an organisation"* (In other words making other's own and drive a BMW while I maintain a bike on EMI). Yet another annoying question used to be" *Are you an MBA?"* Now how could I tell them about my smart calculation of MBA (explained logically in chapter1). So, I would say "Sir actually............." If Goddess Saraswati and luck met together then I used to reach the most fascinating question" *How much do you expect?"* And I wanted to say *"Boss! My worth is more than a diamond mine"* But the words which came out, as if the interviewer had mine Vu doo doll, were" *As per my qualification, skills and job role whatever you deem fit"* Shit!! I said that?

Finally, someone believed in a Non-MBA, graduate, half professional degree guy and offered me a job. With due respect to all those hard-working students who actually cracked good MBA exams, got into good colleges, did summer and all-season internships and got campus placements and all learned and smart engineers, I got a job based on one belief that I cannot move back from here as I didn't had any door behind me as rescue. Next rule – I learned that I can use my tongue, my body language and my communication skills to get a job along with MBA's and Engineer's, and that too when my teachers used to say me *"Sit quietly! Don't be talkative in class!"*

PART B

CHAPTER 1

FIRST JOB

So, dear world, here I am. Energised, excited and enthusiastic and ready to conquer world. Now It's my first day. Entered happily in lift, pushed glass gate and here I was greeted with security guard.." *kaha jaan hai aapko?" And the feeling which I had can't be described in humble words.* Nevertheless, I told him *"I am new joinee here".* Hearing this he smiled and pointed me to a big training room. There I saw many more like me sitting on chair and few standings. *OKZ !! let's gather the strength, and I went in.*

Now here I was given the designation of Agency Manager. At least, I was Manager. Happy? I should be. After all there were people who had done MBA, Engineering, Even Both! And they all were my colleagues. However, the happy feeling of Manager, Cabin, Sipping Tea, Laptop etc. soon faded away, for all. We were supposed to be in field, get business, appoint team, some on pay roll some on pay out basis, motivate them, handle their as well as client queries this all apart from being productive for organisation. Even that was insufficient. The height of injustice was for same target there was different salary due to experience, fresher would get different and those experienced based on last salary drawn. Next Rule – Fancy designation are just a myth. What actually counts is the role and pay out.

The first step of the group upon coming out of shock was go move out of office, go downstairs, order a cut tea and few would add more smoke to environment. For next few months this humble place was going to be our rescue bunker in case of nuclear attacks from our boss, super boss and all great mind of company and of course the motivation centre of self-healing.

Now working here was a different challenge. The boss and super boss from FMCG, seniors who would do business and then there were those who were not doing anything. Then there was I in another dimension which was totally separate from successful and failure people. It's called struggling dimension. I had to attend in house training and even training from outside as and when it was scheduled. The best part was the lunch break.

Sales make you complete man. It demands alertness, forward thinking, happy face, no self-ego, patience, and lot more. I had been student of school of ethical thinking. For me sales meant honest words and honest actions. But to my surprise, I was slowly shifting to failure zone. I also was seeing my colleagues who would change frequently and thus coming out of office every day need to be assured that whether tomorrow I am in the system or not. On top of it, my colleague who was an utter failure in sales magically got the magic lamp. His one of the team mate proved to be a Genie. This gentleman who was about to get fired two months ago now was a hero of branch. His office timing was as per will and all other facilities were provided to him. Even this Genie once banged car of boss in front of me. However only reaction from my boss's mouth was " *He, he, ab apko kya bolu?* Next rule – In sales even one call or one team mate can change the fate. For successful sales man it's life, others follow the rule.

Meanwhile leaning the corporate tactics, I also used to observe around all people in my office. I realized the power of a very uncommon man in my office. He was one of the outsourced housekeeping agency guys. Now this buddy was always smiling and ready to do work. Of course, everyone gave work to him only due to this. Now this buddy used to serve coffee and also help us with banking works. I developed a soft corner for him and made a practice of rewarding him via gifts on festivals and something good occasionally. Result? My clients were always given a VIP treatment in my presence and even my absence. Would also give me office news and even forecast of mood of boss. He would also call me secretly if there was a direct client looking for a help. See? Next rule – Even the bottom end of the corporate food chain can help you out in business. Especially if you are a ready to marry bachelor and your prospective in-laws come secretly to enquire about you in office. Remember? VIP treatment?

Next came the team of people whom I recruited, motivated and pushed for sales. These were from all varieties. And working with them another challenging level of game. These Avengers ensured that not only my left eye but both eyes and both hands as well are damaged. I took targets based upon them. And then they defaulted on the commitments. And then the situation was same as like Guarantor of bank. Now this pile of target pressure was growing inch by inch and this rate it would have grown up more than Mount Everest very soon.

Now in India people are too soft hearted and polite. All those prospective and committed clients to whom I was chasing for last many months would work like a ray of hope. So very confidently I went to meet them and close the deals. One, two, three, four even the last one said" *yes, yes! Yeh product aap se hi lena hai, bus thoda problem hai, baad mein lena pacca hai aapse*" Reason for this *thoda problem* were- "*dhandha manda hai, pitaji se puchna padega, abhi to festival hai, abhi ghumne jaana hai etc*" – Next rule – in sales you will find all shravan kumar only. Interestingly these cute and innocent clients would buy from female sales manager without much questions. And for me it was a solution pending till next birth.

Back to branch fully exhausted and feeling like a child who has lost his pocket money due to a hole in his jeans and even can't complaint to his parents! My boss who was waiting for me to shower his blessings with raised hands suddenly became Thor. His lightning and thunder just shook my inner self and I decided to give one more shot. The best place to visit in such situations was that humble self- healing centre. Now there had been instances of few cases in my own company and other as well where people adopted short tricks to get the business. After all my product was a long-term product. I remember the story of a Khalifa ordering his minister to teach his favourite donkey to read and say else to be hanged till death. However, the minister was brave enough to ask for a fee of 10,000 dinars and all expenses of feeding to be borne by state and a time frame of 10 years. All his wishes were granted. Now when he returned home, his wife shouted at him for being such a stupid and his only reply was" *Don't worry dear! In 10 years either king, or donkey or myself will die to see the consequences*". So, could I do this? The devil and angel played good round of table tennis in my head for quite a few days. At last their ball got lost. And I got the solution. Start again. Build a new team, search again for clients, new areas, do hard work, don't adopt short cuts and this time keep eyes open for new job opportunity as well.

In between all this, the devil of my mind was out for looking for new job and my angel was playing squash alone. Suddenly he gave me an offer of visiting faculty for marketing for MBA in a very reputed private college. Though this proved to be blessing in disguise later.

Teaching was a different experience. More over when most of your students are of same age or few even senior. Must tell you the experience of saying someone that "*you didn't complete your assignment and what you expect in your marks?*" Reminded of old days and a turning of tables. Next rule – Going to gym pays off. At least when you have same age students.

So, between this juggling of my corporate job of learning and another role of being a teacher, my dear devil got me a new job offer. In same field of course but at same pay. Here I remembered the words from one of my trainers of a session in my current company, which I consider the golden rule till yet- *"Never switch job for same role or same package"* I refused the same.

Then as you have critics and dear crab colleagues you also have people who show you how to build a stair from bamboo tree. Here they advised me to go for a corporate certificate. Its industry certificate through an easy exam and makes you fit better in BFSI industry. So, I prepared for it and got it cleared. Why mention this here? Next rule - Staying ahead helps in placing yourself better in future.

So, somehow, I kept optimist and trying and alert, and I got a call for an interview for a different role. Now that's exciting and what I needed. My second job was few steps ahead. Might be or might not be.

CHAPTER 2

SECOND ROLE

Now in my current job I had come to realize the importance of reaching before time hard way. I had to attend the interview in another city and hence wanted to reach on time. So early that I was the first person to reach the place. There I waited for some time and there met a gentleman. I told that I was there for interview but have arrived before scheduled timing. Hence wanted to intimate about my attendance. I was called upon duly at the time of interview and surprise, surprise the gentleman was the interviewer! Now the same story of few questions plus a new *one* "*why did you want to leave your job?*" Can I say I hate my job? Or should I say I am just looking for a change desperately? I somehow thought and replied "*I wanted to change the role as the current role might not offer me a better role as per my ethical thinking.*" Somehow, I was able to explain and convince them with my actions that I meant my words.

Okay then, interview over. And they will let me know the result in some days. Good then let's move back to my city. While going towards the bus stop, sitting in an auto rickshaw got the call from the consultant "*Congratulations! You are selected as the Regional Head for ......area*". Next rule – Miracles do happen. Yes, but the fact that I had team handling experience coupled with my latest industry certificate helped me to gain an advantage over others. Next rule – invest in upgrading yourself. It helps.

In this job, I had another team and bigger area to manage. Yes, this time it was actually manage. I had to travel to meet new clients, handle branch queries, handle client queries as raised by respective team members. Biggest advantage was that this time the Avengers team could not back out with commitments. As I believed in self -development, I made myself good into email communication. So, I could deliver best results in the zone. All good yet. How it can be?

Suddenly one day company had to face regulatory issues and few activities had to be stopped immediately. This impacted the morale of team and also the reputation among clients. Now, again standing to point zero of proving. I recalled the old skills and then tried moulding team to a new product for them and old for me. My previous company product. This helped in boosting the sales to a bit. Few hands here and there, and the team was slowly coming on track. I was more involved in providing solutions through various companies whose products we used to sell. Result- I made good corporate friends. I also got to be involved in region budgeting from head office level. Manpower budgeting, targets, revenue, attending presentations etc.

Sales is a challenging task and being a manager is more than that. Not only one has to manage the team and clients but to manage the boss was another challenge. Here In a short span of five months three bosses changed. And to mould to thinking of each, required another level of patience and self-control. So here starts the level three challenge. My fourth boss was a gem. So big that I can't handle him. By this time, I had earned good reputation and contacts at Head office level. This ensured I came into hate zone of my boss. Now this smart gentleman started making good conversation with my team and few of the *Vibhishan's* allured by my boss started creating headache. Soon this became an ego game between us two with team pulling from both sides. With support from head office I could have easily won the same. However again my school of ethical thinking was seeing discomfort.

As I told you about making corporate friends in this job, I remember sharing this thing with them and out of now where came the thought of getting into training. After all, I had experience of teaching students, had fair command over English and was good in understanding basics. He suggested me to meet his friend in another company same day itself. I did that by noon. That gentleman again told me to meet his senior in same city and check they can do anything. Fine? I tried to control myself and got there. There is met the Regional Head Training and Divisional Manager. After ten minutes of discussion, I was told to wait outside. Now this was getting too much. Finally, the gates opened and here came the cheerful reply" *You are selected, for branch training, at different location and based on you last drawn salary your salary will be higher than your boss, so don't ever reveal that to anyone*" What the ....? At noon I was discussing for job change, after 4 hours I had a job offer. Sometimes things take shape too early. On the basis of this offer I could get rid of this tug of war. Again, the dear old angel and devil played tennis in mind for few days. This time angel won and I decided to quit the job. After all the new job was for different role and different pay. My old admired principle. So, I dig into my personal mails and searched for the resignation letter given to old company and changed the company name and date and send the same through the official email to all.

This resignation letter itself has a story. In my first job (chapter 1), I had made few friends. Now one of my friends was an experienced one and had switched few jobs before joining my previous company. This friend helped in preparing a good resignation letter as it was my first resignation letter. And I didn't want to sound like an award winner actor and two lines quotes. I wanted to avoid any emotional and unnecessary comments in this. So, I took his help and made this near perfect and neutral resignation letter. I used the same in my all job changes and even my colleagues used it as and when they needed it. In today's time I could term it as *'White label resignation letter'*

So dear friends, resignation given and here I deserve a few days break!

Breaks in job may be good but for me who had developed a habit of getting ready in morning to rush to office and travelling through city transport, checking mails and n number of calls daily, sitting idle was another headache. Meanwhile also needed to prepare myself mentally for change of role and even change of city and to convince oneself and family simultaneously is not easy task. The question of future career prospect was also a point as I was moving to a commercially smaller city than I was working and all this create a mist in mind. Meanwhile in between killing days before joining, I got another call a consultant for a job in my own city. What would you do now? Thought a bit and decided to appear for same. If luck favoured then good, else I had a backup this time.

Now this interview was the classic interview of my life. I arrived on time (usual habit), saw few people waiting there in row. I joined with them. Now this was a job in sales and a new industry. Same role in different industry. The feeling of changing the rule was in head. But let's go further. Sometime rules need to be moulded. Now got the call. Entered the cabin and saw three gentlemen on interviewer chair and fourth gentleman along with them in same cabin. Few usual questions and a very strange question from the fourth gentleman *"so are you interested in training?"* Jingle bell, jingle bell, jingle all the way....I said " *yes sir* ". Upon hearing this he said "*wait*" and he went out of the cabin. The rest three told *me" fine then, we were interviewing you for sales and you have said yes for training. So we have nothing to say. You may leave and we will get back to you* "So bit anxious, bit confused I went downstairs and was going towards home. Suddenly got a call from the person who was among the three interviewers that the fourth person wants to meet me. And among all confusions and dilemma, I was selected into training, to handle two states (my back up offered me handling a single branch) sitting in my own city and interesting part was in the group company of my back up plan company!!! *My classic interview, I told you.* So, all what was left was to tell the back-up company not joining them.

CHAPTER 3

TRAINING JOB

Dear folks, it feels good to a sales person if he is not having sales targets and have to guide others. It's a transition from being a player to a coach. All happy yet. Joined the company on the given date though had a slight negative feeling about less package than I thought. But ultimately, I was in the same city or working and it was saving from moving to a different location. First day in job I more like getting introduced and after three days of going and stilling idle and trying to capture things, here enters my new boss. He was Regional Head in Training and I was supposed to report him. Here I was attending his two-day training and was supposed to learn from him by observing him as he was giving training to company associates. In between he used to discuss with me on my experience and preference. After he left for his base location, I was ready and positive about the role. Quite simple? How that's possible? Next day, I got call from the fourth person who interviewed me and he just shouted over phone" *Are you an idiot? Or so confused? I took you for training and then you are saying to your boss, that you are interested in sales. Didn't I ask you your preference in interview?*" Now this raised an alarm and I needed to clear this on urgent basis. I had even closed my back-up door. On top of this I came to know that this fourth gentleman is National Head for

Sales and Training and my super boss!! I was about to faint on this sudden change in weather. Gained back spirits and called super boss from outside the company. Tried to convince him. And got a chance to at least be on ventilator till I prove my worth in the role. From fire to frying pan.

Not losing hope in myself, I was ready to face the things. Then my boss called me up for training session at his base location. This training was the longest even training I had and will do in my entire career. It was for thirty days! I was made to handle and see and work in all departments of that company as if I was a fresher. Too much ego hurt by this time. Moreover, I was supposed the read the product brouchers, manuals, contracts and make a power point presentation on daily basis apart from making the same for the on-job training done in various departments. Same things done again and again till my boss was supposed to be satisfied.

I am a big fan of armed forces. But never thought the same style of training in corporate. And one fine day my boss says *"I have to take a training in your region (previously his region) and you have to watch me and assist me"* Good then. I was ready enough. However, on the appointed date of leaving for the venue, my boss had to cancel his trip and I was told to go alone and do it. Boss, you should have seen the feeling on his face. It was same like a strict mother-in-law reluctantly handling keys of safe to newly-wed bride and challenging her" *now let's see how you manage"* , and me like who had just made some Maggie and small snacks for myself had to suddenly prepare food for a small function of 30 people.

Believing in myself and saying all prayers, I landed in this place and from airport somehow managed to contact the local guy and search for hotel and rest, as it was a Sunday and next day the things will start. Next day dressed in formal, wearing tie (I never had to wear this in my previous jobs) and trying to look matured, got to the branch and introduced myself and then entered into training room. I remember the day when I was entering the same kind of room in my first job and now entering again in different role. Now my corporate friends, corporate training is much different from teaching in class. You have as students', people from different age group, different experience, different mind sets. Some are freshers coming in the financial sector, really excited, some are experienced and ready to do ragging, some are sitting as proxy, clueless for whom to and for what to vote, all with one common interest at least in lunch break – the corporate lunch packets. And to get them all sitting for whole day and keeping them motivated and energised for next day session as well apart from keeping myself motivated and energised to give training that too standing whole day. I was thankful to God; my training was quite well conducted and bit appreciated too. So, after the first hurdle now went to my base location, this time, much confident and ready to take over this corporate ping pong style working.

In this job I had to train all channels of sales and distribution on all products of the company. Slowly the hang of training was looking well. Meanwhile I also had good hands on power point and also started innovating with creative jokes and funny videos to make training sessions bit fun. It started paying off well. Given my sales background, I was also able to deliver on-field training as well. Hence the acceptance was coming fast for me. However, world is never satisfied with what you do. When I was in sales then the statements were" *Sales bahut tough hoti hai na? Tum operations ya training kyu nahi join karne ka dekhte?*" And finally, when I was in training few of the people used to say" *Kyu bhai, Sales kar nehi paate the kya, jo training mein aa gaye?*" I can't describe in words the feeling at those moments. Next rule- You can't satisfy everyone in this world.

Once you handle a large area, Travelling becomes an important area, first of enjoyment and then routine and then concern. I used to travel for a total of 20 days in a month. Normally it could mean travelling for a week at a stretch. At first, I used to enjoy the same. Those days of flight travel when you can boost to your friends about airports and hectic travelling, enjoying varieties of cuisine, good hotels and resorts etc, etc. With all these travelling came good bills of food, hotel, and transport. All my dear corporate traveller friends would be with me in cheering the fact that how much the amount felt short mostly. You ought to be in corporate attire and company won't pay for laundry bills, you had restriction on daily allowance, especially for taxi in case of emergency. Last moment change of travel mode due to non – availability of seats is your headache. Once you manage all this, then you get to your location and the first thing to do is? you guessed right- prepare the travel MIS report, locate and arrange all bills in order and to send the same to boss for his sign and remarks and then wait for amount to land in your account. To manage all this, you take credit card sorry credit cards, and then try to manage the cycle and hope there should not be any deduction. However in between you suddenly remember that you forget to take bill for one or two items or even worse, you have paper bill and the payment proof ink has got distorted due to sweat and all shit. The next tedious task is to remind boss to sign the bills and he is travelling so you have to wait and then the next challenge is to locate and follow with accounts team and their crazy demands. All this, if your courier gets delivered to your head office and from there the guard was sensible to place it on proper desk of the concerned team. Else to fight with entire system with photocopies and to get the claim is liking another Game.

Getting used to all this, was becoming a routine and then it started becoming a concern as I had to eat and drink whatever the dishes were made by the learned chef. Forget what I expected from reading the menu and what I got. I came to discover many colours and sometimes taste of tomato soup across regions. The learned chef would just simply presume the like and handling capacity of tongue to add chillies in food. I was eating so much outside that whenever I reached home and eat healthy food, I used to get stomas ache. Even my family used to get bored in hotels from me as they would go with me and order a dish and I would say *"are, isme yeh aygea, taste dekhna kaisa hoga and etc etc."* It got to that extent that they started avoiding me while going out-side. Even staying in hotel and looking for warm water to a good body retreat post standing from morning till evening sometimes became an unfulfilled wish.

Dress code is another good point in corporates especially when you are in training. So, while everyone might be relaxing in hot summers, I had to keep myself collar up and wearing a tie. And since I was involved in more numbers of training, I couldn't just go with few ties. So, my household budget started to include two or three ties' on monthly basis and soon the number was close to 30. I todays term an investment of close to fifty thousand hang-ing in my closet. The other corporate bug which bite me during tis period was business phone. You can imagine the impression on others if you were using business phones those days. I became so much obsessed with this that I owned all version of Nokia Communicator, yeah dear friends, hope many of you miss it now! Nokia E -series, Blackberry phones, HTC and few other windows phones. Now please don't ask how much money poured in this. Else you will see new river flowing in Indian river map.

Between all these buying selling of phones, ties and all learning and upgrading myself on various products and travelling, one fine day I got the news that my boss has put down his papers. I must be happy then. As in six months review cycle, I had to miss the bus as I was a grade below than my colleague on the same package just because my Boss had forgot to upgrade my Grade at the time to my joining!! Felt so much anger though tried to control I was still enjoying the job and felt that may be in I next cycle all will be sorted out and as committed by my boss.

Happiness is not ever lasting. I was supposed to report the other regional trainer. He was among the three national level trainers along with my boss. Again, started same story of travel bills, com-mitment though in different voice and tone. By God's grace my performance as a trainer was being appreciated by my respected super seniors and even the branch sales head and sales team as well. This was a great motivational factor to keep me motivated to go ahead. Came another cycle of promotion. This time got the chance but again the previous commitments were not fulfilled. Next rule – New boss new carrots. I was again getting frustrating on this. On top of this, one fine day when I went home from tour, my elder daughter who was just six months old then, started crying as soon as I took her in my arms as if I was some stranger! What the hell is this? I am doing so much work and even handling carrots just to see this? Nope, never. This incident just shook me and I decided to what I have been doing earlier. Switch job! So, started thinking on this and started searching job through consultant and corporate network as well. Luckily my network connects magic worked and dear readers I got a new job again. This time got a very, very good hike and also good position. So happily, informed the seniors and this time also refused all proposals of staying and changing the profile, no carrots and no other vegetables please. And here again used my "white label resignation letter"- Remember search mail, Download, edit company name and send. Easy..

CHAPTER 4

NEW JOB

The present job offer was quite lucrative. I got a bigger area and grade in company and the hike was too good. Of course, here two the rule applied- Don't switch on same role same package. So dear friends, it was a different product in BFSI industry and the role was in Sales. Sales? Yes! you read it right. I was back in sales though this time at different level and role. The job offer was referred through an ex-boss whom I pay regards till today as well. Corporate connections pay fruits. This company was a new company formed post-merger of a PSU controlled company and an MNC. So, you can imagine the culture difference apparent between old team and new team.

Though In terms of team size it was just me and five persons responsible for handling two states entire sales and support. This meant team doesn't necessarily means a whole regiment. It can be only three or five as well. Nevertheless, the product was to be sold through various distributor channel only, hence the team was sufficient to handle the same. Now in this role I couldn't say that *"underperformance of branches is not my concern."* It was my area and I was the profit center head and I had to deal with it. Now I came to realise the situation of my earlier bosses. They had to commit before bosses and then deal with team and prove that they are a worthy leader. Same feeling of the patty in between two slices of a burger. Pressure from both ends. However, I had to take hard steps related to team in downsizing. Even in appointments I relied on reference from an old corporate friend and past performance of the candidate. This proved well for some time though I feel that I should have checked the persons interest while asking for reference. Next rule- You need to recheck the corporate friend's interest. A friend few years ago may switch sides later.

Coming to the sales channel. In this industry distributors were not as a regular franchisee or dedicated distributors like any other FMCG industry. These distributors were like a freelancer who can distribute products of all companies that were operating in my current industry. Now imagine the situation. I had to present my company, my products, my offers, support them with budgets, handle the entire support system on single call and that too without any commitment of business and even surety of business. The product will be thought of, if it's performing well in the market which was managed by an entirely different team sitting on a very high level in head office. Then it should be supported by sales commission and an additional budget which again was in control of Head office, I had a very little say in this. Then came the task of supporting the client's and the distribution channel. And that too for those persons, to whom I cannot force to sell my product only. I developed a great respect for people from pharma sales as the work was same just at a bit different level and industry. Though they have stockist to at least support in month end, in case. Here in my current industry the client can call us to get the product return at any time and we can't refuse buy back. So, in nut shell it was more like managing distribution channel expectations and doing all good to ensure client retention and simultaneously hoping for goof performance of product so that sales target can be taken based upon that. The best rule to judge whether my offer was good or bad was through a small signal which I saw at a distributor's place. If the offer was good, he would offer a bowl of cashew, almonds and pistachio. If it was not good for him, he would offer a bowl of candy. Next rule – In business, you are praised for what you can offer instantly. Not what you can generate later.

In this job I also learned a new technique of sharing one sided-knowledge and even the good old whole class punishment, "Con-call". A magical word by just dialling few numbers on telephone pad with speaker ON, so that everyone in the team can listen whole dictionary of alien words from the product team and then asked for *"how to pitch and sell"*, another voice would come from our sales head" *For this we will have another concall"* Some days I felt like our respected *Sunny Paaji* " *Concall pe concall, concall pe concall"*. Though it was nothing compared to what my dear friends in telecom industry have to face. My deep regards to them for facing this concall system. And as I became more acquainted to concall, I realized the power of mute button in phone and having a Bluetooth in ear. Boss, concall on! You switch on Blue-tooth, put the call on Mute and listen to all good music in car in high volume while you drive to office or chill yourself in a café reading some online article. After gaining this enlightened know-ledge about product and about Indian industry and government trends coupled with global trends as well, we used to go and meet distributors charged. And discuss all this global *gyan* sipping cup of tea and the answer to final question- *"Sir, fir is mahine kitna contribute karenge"* was humble polite and with a smiling face- " *Bat-eate hain, karna to hai"*. Next rule – global *gyan* is worthless if the product can't be sold.

In life the three most important necessity are *roti, kapda aur makaan*. In my industry to sell, the most essential basic neces-sity were pen, diary and calendar. *"Yeh nahi to samjho Jeevan nahi"* Now my company was an MNC, hence question of these things didn't arise. For them generating returns, product information brochure and concall were good. Result was obvious. The sales was like an Olympic marathon with only difference was in that in my lane there we hurdle where-as for my peers in other companies it was smooth lane. The only dedicated channel was the tie up with our parent company which was a nationalised bank. Here also to get the work done without any incentive was different task. Forget about product pitch. The training to staff and getting all on one level was through a series of permission and meeting up to regional level. On the training days the protocol needs to be followed. Welcome speech, then contents, then thanks word. Most importantly the tea and snacks. And the situation when I used to come to know that the previous head of the branch or region or even the field person whom we trained as been transferred in mid. Like you play Ludo and are knocked out in between and then to start again.

Now as far as products performance goes, the real challenge is not the product alone. It's the industry as a whole. In this job I got to know the same in hard way. The industry was booming at such a level that each investor would earn such a huge amount that they were ready to switch companies for various products in a span of three or four months. However, all this came to a sudden halt. When I joined the industry looking a good opportunity there was a sudden downfall across global sector. The Indian markets were down by almost seventy percent from the peak level during a period of twelve months. And to hold the clients and face their queries and meeting distributors and staying positive were typical concerns. However, as good days don't stay for long so as bad days also don't stay for long. Things improved slowly for betterment of all. Next rule – you may be too smart but to be the right person at right time is what is called luck in sales.

During these job after seeing up and down in job, the bug of entrepreneurship had bitten me deep. This time I myself organised the table tennis match between angel and devil and invited them to play. The strength of confidence, sales experience, availability of credit limits, and even loans due to good salary was enough to shift the inclination towards own set up. I didn't want to pursue in the same field. Instead wanted to follow my creative skills and wanted to make a livelihood in different sector. In between all this dilemma and confidence, I arranged for loan as working capital, took a place on rent, got few interiors done and bough the materials to sell. Took a risk and I thought I could manage it along with my family members. Which though didn't work well. Next rule- your family may support you but they are working along with you is different situation.

And when the times comes it doesn't come alone. My boss who had hired my had left the organisation and even the top management had changed. New boss was from a different sector though in financial only. Soon I stared seeing changes in team, old person in system getting replaced by new ones at a fast pace. I was having a feeling that my number could come soon. It's known as corporate war among peers. My decision to get into business was also influenced by the same sense. At this point when I was having tug of war with my boss, one of my old corporate friends who had previous connection with my boss was able to change the situations. He too was in my industry only in other company and there was trouble going in his company as well. He was aware of my business plans and also the discussion I was having in my company. So, the best strategy he adopted was to back stab me and replace me. Next rule-A friend in need may instead put you in need. Choose your friends wisely.

So, this time the resignation was just a formality and to tell yourself and family that from next day the things are not usual takes its on courage. Still I had hope for my business.

CHAPTER 5

BUSINESS BUG

I had started business by opening a store and I felt that it will work and since I have sales experience, I was confident. I also hired a staff for assisting me. Few days it was doing fine. Going on field and meeting clients is altogether different from sitting at one location and waiting for them. To get me out of boredom I installed music system in store at least to keep myself energetic. There were occasional customers as well. It was a routine till the time my staff told me that he won't come due to personal reasons. And this came as a shock. He was trust worthy and old known to me. Moreover, the location was proving me too hectic and managing alone was getting bit odd. So, I decided the switch location. I choose the location close to my residence so that I can manage the same easily. And in new place I had also to alter the stock. People here wanted different products. Thankfully this time I rented a place of my friend who also operated the next shop. At least I was not going to get bored. Though I also had installed games on my laptop to keep me alive during waiting period of client. I hope I played the games long after Mario, Contra and sometimes it was so relaxing. This friend of mine would give me good tips on managing stock, buying the types of products and even help me in locating the suppliers.

Things started settling slowly. I was getting repeat customers and also new people used to visit the store, enquire and sometimes buy too. However, there were two major challenges I was facing apart from capital. First- dress code. Imagine, you are accustomed of wearing well ironed sober shirts tucked in with neat trousers, sleeves down with cuff links and polished shoes and a scent and to have to sit in a retail store waiting for clients. Wearing causal or even the traditional on weekdays was an alien habit to me. Even though I tried to cope up with this, the second challenge was more tough. To sit on a chair all day long and count stock and even arrange and rearrange them and wait for clients (it was a new store, remember?). It was not my cup of tea. I had been conditioned for a different style of working.

After thinking for alternatives and various trial and errors I finally decided to use the old style of door to door sales instead of sitting in one location. I recollected the memories of one gentleman who used to sell tie by visiting corporate office and I had met him during my visits in one of my branches in my earlier job. So, I took some products which I believed were sellable, tucked them in a large bag, put the bag in my car and I went off to sell it to corporate offices. Though, I didn't go to the people I knew so that I can save the laughs upon me. As they won't understand the reason behind this.

I met one of the team leaders in a call center and gave him a free gift and he arranged to pitch my product to his team and will tell them to meet me at parking premises and that I can offer a good deal on those products. Touchwood this worked well. Within just two hours I managed to sell good numbers at a good profit. I was happy! And this bought a sign of relief. I started focusing on this and would ensure that at least in a week I do so. However, this stared effecting my store as now people would not see me in store, as I was busy selling somewhere else. But I started liking the same as It was like my old days with just change of product. But the challenge of blood of business remained intact. Money was not as per my expectations and my EMI plus the expenses were not as per the income. I was reducing fast on cash and my savings. I needed to plan for alternative soon.

So, deciding on my limitation of capital and sitting capacity and a flair for corporate style working I changed my business product. Call it resignation again but this time the sender and recipient were same. I changed the business, packed and dumped all left-over products after sales discount at my home (few still are there used as decorative show pieces). This time I connected with my relative and started doing corporate sales. I decided to pursue creative skills into space design and entered into furniture. There was good profit in first deal itself and boss! this I what I needed. So much that I again changed the location of the store and converted it to my office and kept few products as sample.

Now I could approach my old corporate friends and few known persons and present the business and ask for reference as well. Which I did. I was getting good contracts. It was similar to my style. Dressing up in corporate, dealing with good people and also money was good. I was loving it and enjoying the work. Here the challenges of capital and people management were different. As I was moving up the ladder the capital requirement to initiate the project and procure the material and also to pay for labour and get the pay out in stages needed to be met. The team here were all different than the team I used to work with. Blue collar team has different style of working. The word 'time commitment' is on the least priority for them. Further when they know that you have less product knowledge, chances of nuisances increase. I was get-ting more and more contracts and to manage capital and people and even suppliers was a tedious task. I was well dressed, well-mannered, but in this line the language and style were different. And to test the capacity of my mental and financial strength, two of my big clients stopped the last instalment of payment owing to delay in work. This sudden halt of capital and commitment to pay the dues to supplier and the working team further pushed me to the grave. I was entangled in this situation coupled with the fact of remaining dues of EMI and cards etc.

Now I was left with two choice- to again raise capital from other sources and pump in to business. I was having old and new clients and things could settle in some days, hope so. Or to plan for a bold step. I was struggling with business for last two years and a half-year and eroded almost all my saving and had created new liabilities as well. The idea of raising fresh capital and to again wait for things to turn over didn't suited me. After discussing with own and near ones for almost two months and recalculating all pros and cons I decided to move out of business and look for a job. I can't just go on living like this my whole life. I needed the get the things back on track.

CHAPTER 6

JOB AGAIN

The decision to move back to job was very difficult for me. First of all, to prepare myself mentally to accept the fact of failure and to remain calm was very tough task. Second most difficult task was to search for suitable job as I had been out of job connect for three years. Even to get the desired package was not an option because of the break and everyone tries to take advantage of it. But I was determined this time and hence decided to start afresh with new challenges. This time my corporate connects again worked out and I was referred for a job in automobile industry. This was an altogether different sector for me. But somehow my interest in automobile and luck favoured me. I was selected and preferred even above the internal candidates. Though it was a fresh start again in terms of package but at least I will be getting steady income.

Here I was supposed to handle a team of fifteen people and was responsible for overall sales, finance collection and customer satisfaction for the vehicle segment given. This vehicle was new launch and already created a hype in market. To the extent- that before launch we had more than two hundred bookings unofficially and near about eighty booking after official booking announcement. Irony was we were allotted only thirty to forty vehicle per month by the company.

So, when you are flooded with sales it's a matter of joy. Right? I must say no. It must be matched with stock availability as well. To hold client bookings was a herculean task for me. My team will simply put the queries to me and I had less control on things. Another challenge was everyone wanted vehicle in first chance. I never witnessed a thing like this in my life. People made this vehicle as status symbol. And getting the vehicle was a must for them. I was lured for cash and was even threatened for life if I would not deliver the vehicle! Even I got request as silly as *"Vehicle jaldi chahiye. Bacche ne college jaane se mana kar diya hai"*. In another instance" *Mera beta shaadi ki date aage badaane ka bol raha hai agar gaadi nahi mili to"*. On top of it another was" *I had promised my wife for a trip to Goa by this car. I need to save my marriage"*
Amidst all these, pressure and excitement, we somehow managed to get high allocation owing to number of bookings and we got eighty vehicles in first lot. Good to hear that? Boss, I had close to three hundred bookings with everyone promised first delivery. This time my seniors who had good experience in this, showed me ways and also helped me out in regaining the control and confidence to manage the show.

Now my friends in automobile will relate to the experience of maintaining demo vehicles, arranging test drives, taking bookings, maintaining the showroom vehicle, to pitch accessories, get the initial documents for finance, arrange and prepare the vehicle for delivery, preparing the file, getting all clearances, the delivery process, and the after sales feature demo and to follow with financers for dues and lastly to send the papers for registration and getting the registration number. All this for one client. Think! we had more than three hundred.

For next three months it was all chaos in the premises. People would flood in to see the vehicle and those who anticipated delivery they used to come and shout, and those who got delivery were so impatient to allow us to follow thorough processes. And then one of enthusiast driver, (In India, we don't need F-1 tracks. There all type of people doing same with their regular vehicles in busy roads all day) accidently damaged one demo vehicle and I was left with one to manage the show. This demo vehicle was put for repairs. Though It never came out from repair. As whenever the sales team used to fall short to replace the defective item in ready to delivered vehicle, they will take the parts from this vehicle. This vehicle transformed from demo vehicle to donor vehicle.

In India festivals are a great day of joy and celebration. In my school days, I had written many essays on festivals of India and on special days of life. However here I felt the pain of other side of table. Since this job, I have developed a great respect and honour for all people working in retail and automobile and even transports who will sacrifice their festive day to make other feel the enjoyment and happiness. Now to manage the delivery "*as per muhurat*" was another task. Every client had different auspicious time. Some will share the same timing. And then to get the vehicle delivered was a team task. The most stressful were odd hour and week off delivery. On these times we didn't had seniors to approve the delivery and to manage the delivery experience used to be a bit negative feedback.

Among all these things slowly the mad craze for the vehicle was fading way. Hence, we were supposed to start thinking on new lines of sales. I was performing better than my counter parts as my sales and the collection was very good. We never had outstanding for more than a week and it was all in control. Working with near about three hundred people on same place with all level of hierarchy was different experience for me. However, at this people bandwidth instances of slippages and leakage in system ought to be there. I didn't belong to that practice. I was shaped and trained to be productive and not looking for such leakage for personal benefit. Hence, I started looking for role expansion and also to control the leakage. I thought that this would be appreciated by my boss and seniors. However, they were reluctant to this. I was in job but had tasted business blood. Hence, I had a different mindset to look at things. I even told this matter in different language to the respective owners of the organisation. But all in vein. And to be very clear I had failed in business but didn't wanted to grow in job as I had now business mindset and it meant failure was just another experience. I had to rectify my mistakes and prepare myself thoroughly for second inning.

Working here was fine. I was having a nice time. I was ready to work and again prove the skills so that they had to give me role expansion to be more productive. However, one fine day saw two new seniors above me. They were new to organisation but old in industry. Old in industry is good for many people however I has also proved myself in last one year and I had my previous experience with me. I was liking our respected Anil Kapoor ji in *Nayak* movie." *Mein politics mein ek saal se hu par tum se ladte ladte mera tajurba eiktis saal ka ho gaya hai"*. So dear folks I was happy to use my old weapon – my favourite resignation letter and to join a new role in new company. Next rule- you fear for failure only once.

CHAPTER 7

BACK TO INITIAL

The new job which I got was in my previous industry before business. Though again the golden rule applied. Never switch on same package same role. So, I switched sides. I joined a distribution firm. Here I was supposed to interact with clients and thus I ensured that this time I was on the commitment side and my earlier colleagues were on request side. But here was the challenge. I had never interacted with direct clients in my career profile. Hence this was a new and tough for me. But at this stage now the things were supposed to be different. I was supposed to leverage my knowledge and experience and prove myself.

So, I learnt the technique of interacting with direct clients and slowly started delivering up to the expectations.

In this job, the first thing was the setup of a very small office. Any one from corporate won't even think of joining there. However, thanks to my business bug, I knew that whatever size the place of office is, it's your place of livelihood and it must be respected at all cost. Though in times to come I was allowed to change the feel of infrastructure of office and eventually the office grew in size.

Thankfully the team was good. Team meant two support staff

and together we were managing the show. Now the team was very much older than me in system. That meant they had old ways of dealing with clients. In service industry you cannot ignore the importance of upgrading with the times and in some cases, you have to be a pioneer to get along with the rising expectations of client. So, it was fun to train the team. To upgrade them to email communication language, phone etiquettes and ensuring client experience while their visit to office was bit frustrating alongside fun as well. Even to upgrade the team to online mode which was an upcoming trend in financial services was a tough task. And in between experimenting with old team and new team was a regular task, but few stayed for long and alongside old team the entire team slowly became an asset.

Dealing with direct clients and meeting their expectation is not easy. One has to be patient and also have to be tactful in replying. As one theory for a client won't be applicable for another client. Even for same client the theory will change as the market conditions changes. This tactfulness was also needed for holding client with companies. Another important word which I realised was commitment and also speaking true conditions in services. It may sound odd but it makes life easier. And to answer every query of client was like next to impossible. But looking for solutions upgraded the skills and hence helped in long term.

In financial services or any other services industry, operations becomes an important role. The client will give the form at his place or at your office. Then to arrange the same, fill the same properly, ensuring the proper supporting documents alongside and to make the form available to be processed further is itself a tedious task. But this is what is the service industry about. Even how to use the docket boy effectively is an art sometimes. As these resources are much limited in an organisation and has everyone bossing them, to get the things done in proper time-lines calls for a different skill set.

Now in small set up office another challenge is of the IT infrastructure. You need to bear with low end configuration and also have to bear with old age software for dealing with data. Now in financial services industry, data is important however other important part is internal MIS. I was accustomed to look at MIS, shoot emails and make strategy to overcome the hurdles and look for ways to stick on track. Here the task was to make the mistake, shout on self, try to self-motivate and then again get on foot and try making things good. For me laptop was an important accessory till this job. Here to live with desktop was something annoying. However, this helped my pitch to improve. And in time to come this also was taken care of.

Now dear friends, this job was more like having own business. So, I finally started to upgrade myself in terms of knowledge. My understanding on costs and benefit and volume based on my previous experience of business helped me stay in this job for near about six years. Yes! you heard right dear friends. This long journey was all possible due to the variety of experience I had in my entire career journey till date. And I was keen on getting into business again. Hence this opportunity was a boon for me in identifying the gaps I had and also the reasons for failure of my business. So, I am planning to use my white label asset for one more time in home that the things will first get bit shaky at first and then in control in time to come.

With this, the journey of the career experiences comes to a stage of confident and experienced tag. The next part will be an interesting part to read as I will summarize all experienced and collected and gathered moments which shape oneself from the initial days of career to future days of responsibilities. Hope the learning will be useful to all fresh graduates, in process- managers, to know the skills and tact's in advance and for experienced people a recall of sweet and sour memories.

PART C

Evolution skills

1. Casual is good but formal is better

Once we get job, the first problem is wardrobe. Problem? Yeah! As a student we prefer tees and jeans and cool hairstyles. Tattoo is *IN* now -a-days. But in corporate world, *formals* is the language. Ensure to invest in at least two or three formal dresses in last year of college. Cool hairstyle's must be given a time being bye-bye. However, its subjective to the profession. The attire makes a difference. People normally presume sincerity and attitude by seeing. Hence ensure to look well and descent especially if you are in profession of discussing money matters.

But this formal wear policy doesn't mean you cannot be relaxed. Thank God! We have Fridays and Saturday's in week. Mostly companies allow you to be relaxed on this days and casual are allowed. However, for me the interesting part was to first buy formals post my appointment and then to think later after some time that company should make a dress code. At least I could have saved the pain of thinking each night what to wear next day. Too much thinking and asking to God for repeated things usually result in him listening the same. So, at a point in my life I used to wear dress code and it included white shirt and coat to wear. Think of a sales person who has to go on calls using all modes of transport and wearing white shirt and coat! Next rule – Always pray logically.

Another important thing is to look descent. I would avoid word like masculine, lean, smart, beautiful, etc. I am emphasising on descent. It meant for me to choose attire that would complement me to make the impression better and thus would help me in winning visual trust of the other person. For looking descent during the whole day is a challenge. I am not saying of face dullness which you can just make fresh via a simple wash. I am talking about corporate saviour kit. My colleagues used to call this a vanity kit and my car as a vanity van. My saviour kit included a shoe shiner, wet wipes, hand sanitizer, mouth freshener and handy deo. This kit ensured that I looked well charged at even odd hour of meeting and most often after reaching client's place after a hell lot of road adventure. It also saved calls if I had to meet clients due to sudden urgency post my booze party. Though in my vanity car I used to keep additional dress for saving the day from misfortune and a pair of shoes esp. in rainy season. One final line it's always Man vs. Client.

2. Don't fear high educated. Trust skills

When I joined the first company, I was afraid of not being MBA. But the essence is You just need to trust your skills. For any job in corporate you require to have good communication skills and clarity in your mind where to go. Eventually you will find ways how to go for sure. In sales or any other function how, you perform and what you deliver matters. The ultimate *gyan* in corporate is to apply what you have learned. Unfortunately, it seldom happens. Remember! The degree is just a gate pass to enter. The stair to success is through your performance and use of skills. You cannot upgrade your skills through software download. I learned this thing hard way and also made a point to rely upon oneself as this is the base of future growth.

It's also interesting to note that these skills were very basic skills however I used to ignore them sometimes. It could be due to arrogance or over confidence. The skills are quite simple – To know when not to speak and when not to react. These looks very simple but to practice them in daily life made me much better in terms of dealing with various category of people.

3. Working in Agency Distribution

The aim is to build a team that will work for you and get rewards and recognitions apart from remuneration. *Reality is – you may be superman and can lift whole mountain but to tell others to move a piece of stone is another task.* Identifying right person with skills, talent, willingness to earn extra and justified excuses for not-working is the right strategy. To have team of such people is the ultimate *moksha*.

So how do you find your Avengers? Usually people prefer the natural market and it means approaching to those persons whom you know in your friend circle, relatives, acquittance etc. The strategy works well if this person is already into the business of distribution especially in the industry you are doing job. Else approaching new prospects is a better long-term idea.

Now there is a chance if you are in financial industry and the person whom you are approaching and no agreed says you to bear the initial exam cost or likewise. Personally, I feel that if any businessman can't expend some amount on own then he or she is not that serious for business. The major thing to identify is not the contact list of the person and not even willingness to earn. Everyone has at least four hundred numbers in cell phone and similarly everyone is happy with money coming in account. The major and most important thing is to check for willingness to go to people and pitch business without any hesitation or reservation. Next rule – A person who doesn't takes pride in his business may not be that successful.

The agency team should be from various background and locations so that you can take full advantage of the concept of law of average. Everyone will not perform at all times, however you might get average business on regular business. Next step is to ensure that they have proper product and process knowledge. It's important, as the same is transferred as per self-understanding to clients. And hopefully you won't want them to bother or knock you for every matter. The product and process knowledge are also helpful in pitching the product rightly as you are in a position to know the depth and extent of sales and services commitment.

Now the next question is whether this team will survive and will perform every time? The answer is NO. The team will first grow at very fast pace and then will go to a sudden halt making you revolving head to toes. The best part is to realise that the team is not your direct subordinates or team mates. They are with you for a purpose which will shift if their focus shifts. Hence you cannot use pressure and targets system. It has to be request and soft style approach. Second important thing to realise is that team members will shift focus or may find another offer. Hence the constant task in motion should be to always look for new prospective team members, train them and try selling through them.

In FMCG/Telecom/Pharma or any other industry the agency model is different. The person has invested a good amount in infrastructure, team and stock. Sometimes the distributor/agency is financial much stronger than it looks upfront. So, the key point is to handle the same carefully.

In all cases, you might have the authority and power to dissolve the agency contract but remember you are in field for business and also you might need the same distributor in another job. The other important thing to remember is the ageing and profitability of the agency in the system. The agent/distributor might be old in the system and might have been allocated to you. He may be much experienced in process than you and also might have seen numbers of managers handling his agency. Don't try to act over smart here. Try to remain as natural and possible and stick to commitments which you can fulfil. Later when you get in gel with the agency then make relaxed working. The profitability has also to be checked and respected. This way you will be able to make more better judgements in terms of making business strategies for team.

4. Self-learning. Less dependency on seniors

This is quite hard to digest. As when we are students then things were easy and handy for us and suddenly in job market we are thrown in front of lions. So, its better to learn loading and firing own guns rather than hiding in shadow of some saviour. Your first job may be a welcome note for you and your family but the actual fact is that you have indirectly created a competition for the existing team and hence very few people will be willing to share their experience and teach you the skills. This would have been less dramatic had we would have taken internships seriously which seldom happens. The problem gets bigger when you have got the job because of a reference.

So dear friends, please don't assume spoon feeding. The only thing which will helped me in this is – clarity of role. This automatically guided me to connected path of learning the basic and skilled tricks. Even the place of storing file, having a copy of required forms, having a knowledge of making coffee from machine, photocopy, system network resolution, etc will helped a lot apart from the bigger things like product and process knowledge and raising queries for better understanding of clauses and developing pitch for better sales figures. You might find this a silly matter, but in long run this approach helps in always looking for fine details and equips in reading between the lines.

This self- learning also ensured that I finally developed to a stage where the whole office was centred around me. It also helped me later in my career as I was able to train my team better and also ensured that I made good systems and process in office.

5. Office relations

You might be very good in social media and having good followers online but staying in job and getting promoted and referred for other job is different media. Even your best friend or family member might not be able to help you in getting a job or job growth or switch. Next rule- Maintain corporate networking. You have to understand the approach of dealing with three main levels. These are seniors, colleagues and juniors. The various sublevels have their own importance and expectations.

Seniors include your immediate reporting senior and super-senior and channel head and other departments seniors and respective heads. Don't confuse your boss with Tom Lee Jones in Men In Black. He has his own work and more numbers of "J" under him. Getting too friendly and personal might create tensions later in job. Do this at your own risk. This also holds true if you have good relation with super boss as you might be his reference, but remember to give due respect to you immediate reporting senior. You never know when you might again face your boss in next or future assignments. So, try to be honest with your immediate boss as he knows your daily activities and limits far better than other seniors in institution. Your immediate senior helps you in staying steady in job and if he is good, then you can face every storm and thunder and rain by standing under his umbrella. You can be assured of getting job as and when he switches or at least finding a job in emergency situations. Best of luck for the good relations. However, the chances are also that this gentleman proves to be a devil in your life. How do you know this? - is through observing the behaviour towards you during multiple occasions and instances. If he is good then he will always support you in time you need that and will defend you when time demands so. Respect him even if he is strict and demanding in job as this person will ensure you learn well and grow in life eventually. However, working under devil boss may be injurious to career and health as well. This gentleman will ensure you mostly suffer in terms of reward and recognitions. What this does? It kills your zeal and enthusiasm. In frustration you do mistakes which are then used against you. It's an old corporate saying – "People don't leave companies they leave bosses". So, you can mostly blame this gentleman if you had to switch job earlier than thought of.

However, being in good books of your super senior will help you in your career strategically. Firstly, because of the authority he has in your current organisation and secondly in looking for an elevated opportunity as and when this gentleman switches his role. With his access to much large group of people he definitely is in a better position to offer something good for you. So, always try to maintain a smooth professional relationship with this position and person in particular.

Your colleagues are the next level to focus on. However, the sub level can be experienced or fresher like you or even younger to you. The people who are in same role as of you will be definitely good for you as an office stress buster. You might also eventually become good personal friends in due course of time. A twin advantage! The reason for maintaining a good relationship in spite of they being your competitor is in future roles. They will grow with you and when you will be in a different role and sectors this cross-industry relationships helps you in flying over the traffic jam of servicing hurdles. They are also helpful in giving you or recommending you the junior team as and when you may require the same to be hired.

Your juniors are good team mates. You must maintain a good relationship with them. Even a office boy will be useful in serving coffee/tea first to you apart from helping you get alerts about office grapevine. Your team is those persons who share your targets and help you grow. Hence have sense of praise for them. And maintain good relationship, if possible, post job as well. You might don't know when you will go to a next level in job and then again you need reliable team.

Apart from same you might also have to interact with people from other departments at all levels as the situation demands. Now since you might not have to see them or interact with them often, you can have bit liberty to not maintain much in depth relations. However, if you are smart enough to judge future then a word of advice is to maintain relationship with them as well. It again helps when you see them in your new role in future and also that they can be a good source for reference for team recruitment and also in case you need to refer someone.

6. E mail – LOL

Nice slang word used in chatting. And then there are emojis as well. All these words come from a different language dictionary of social media. But dear friends, please remember you are in business culture and better to revise some rules of grammar and also of English words as spelled in Oxford dictionary.

You might have to write a letter to colleagues, but mostly is reply to seniors, clients and instructions to juniors. Now here your sense of communication should be good enough to make a good impression. Cautious advice – don't use synonyms and antonyms. You are here for official work not for taking English Language classes. Most important skill is – to make the reader understand what you wanted to convey with full clarity. You may use help of screenshots, attachments, bullet points etc. But please don't write essays on mail.

The most dangerous thing is replying on email. Usually we use the same while driving and in hurry. And in turn result in sending few mails to unwanted seniors. I had seen my few colleagues being victim of this stupidity.

Another irritating thing is trail mail. Very often people use this technique of referring to old communications as a reference. However, this becomes a mess when there are too many recipients in the mail and everyone is having a group debate on email. A simple tip is to copy the trail mail in a file as attachment if someone is interested in archaeological discovery of facts. Another word of precaution is to see whom you are replying to. Reply all is good however sometimes may turn up against you.

When writing to a client the most important point is to understand that you are now replying to someone outside your company. Hence anything you say, commit or deny can be used against you. So please refrain using any offensive language. And also try to keep the matters to seniors in case you have to reply to a client who knows them just to ensure that your seniors understand that you are in touch with client for his query.

Last but very important advice. If you are living in India, then please call to the recipient of mail that you have send the mail as desired. Trust me, it will save much pain later.

7. Office social media groups and pages

In today's time this has become an important channel of re-porting and among colleagues' groups as mode of pouring own thoughts in public. This mode is the most dangerous mode. It's like a kid driving a car on busy road. Chances of accidental post are too high. I had witnessed my few colleagues forwarding fun messages on reporting groups. Though they were still connected with me outside office post this event. I always avoided using or texting in reporting two groups simultaneously and especially during hurry or taking risk while driving (please stop this prac-tice if one is still having this habit). Though I must admit this fun group is a great office stress buster.

The reporting groups can be or I must say, mostly are quite irritat-ing owing to the continuous post on the group. The balanced and experienced mind people do avoid late night post. However, the problematic is over enthusiastic and freshers (we called them by many names). The continuous ping of this group was too annoy-ing especially at nights and when I was having a week off or on leave. This reporting group helped me in becoming a more stable mind person. How? Simple I never used to get excited or troubled when some posted about business and when our bosses used to reply in either ways on those posts. This is which I called Corpor-ate Experience Nirvana.

The situation is more dangerous on social pages of company. I used to refrain from pouring my active thoughts of like and com-ments mostly. I used to do so only on common matters that too like standing in last line and singing in chorus. These common matters are launch of new product, celebrating some events etc.

This will make life much hassle free. The more precaution must be taken while posting on any other pages or groups of public especially when someone is authorised to handle company pages. I would even avoid commenting to any post using my company name. I have my liabilities to be taken care of. This thought is the best self-control before getting excited to post a reply.

8. Certifications

It's a good chance that you got selected in job may be after completing higher secondary, graduation or post-graduation. But don't underestimate the power of certifications. I am talking about industrial certifications and continuous learning programs. These actually helps in staying connected with the latest trends and also helps in bring future closer to you bit fast than other people. You might always want to be industry ready not to grow but also to survive.

These certifications had helped me in getting better jobs as I was equipped with the right skills which industry required. It also helped me in enhancing my image of always looking for upgrading which is seen as a good sign or corporate culture. This also helped me in winning confidence of the clients as they knew that I have the experience as well as the desired knowledge to interpret the clauses better than few others. Next rule- job is a step career is a very long journey burdened with expectation of many people on you alone.

9. Presentation – Use of MS office to win in office

You might have used systems or phone for all productive and personal purpose but having good knowledge of using twin swords of Ms office will make you the respected office samurai for all times. Master the swords and you will see your life changing for all time. Now for me I remember myself going to computer coaching institution for a diploma certification. In those days, it was a must and cool learning skill.

However, fighting in arena in video games is different from real world. So, this dear computer used to make my work tedious. The number of reports we need to prepare and also the urge to keep database, finally forced to find a way out. That was to master the skills. Now what to master first. Normally at base level of job more need is to fill data in the required sheet. So, the simple thing was to first ensure speed in typing. Post this the next logical step was to ensure correctness while data input. After getting good in data entry the next step was to find some shortcut to fill the data in much speedy manner. That's where the DNA of *Jugad* boils up in the blood. So, tried digging in and got few formula and short tricks which made the task easy.

This short trick is good when you have to be at base level. But as you move up the ladder, the sheet remains the same. Your vision changes. The same thing happened to me when I was raised up in corporate ladder. The challenge here was not only feeding the data but also to edit sheets of team. The important thing to understand was how to analyse the data and to maintain records for future reference. This is certainly not an easy task. In bigger corporation one can enjoy luxury of dedicated MIS person. But in smaller companies this task comes to the senior itself.

Now I could also rely upon junior who would prepare the data for me and I can name it. But the issue was I can not share the data of other executives with him and also that his vision for analysis was definitely aligned to me. Even if I managed this issue the problem was that this forwarding of data would put in trouble in front of my seniors.

The other alternative was to develop myself in same. This however will make my work more cumbersome. Not only I had to see what they have written, but to also had to communicate with team simultaneously and had to correct their inputs. Now I came to know how my teachers felt when they had to check our copies in exams and also to give marks! I also had to fill in my data sheet. But this all pain was for some time only. I later realised this hard work helped me in gaining speed in terms of analysis and helped in plotting good image.

The second most important office system skills is knowing use of Power point. The name is a goof fancy name. As a college student the ppt made are very extensive. For one topic we used to make a ppt of about thirty to forty slides. But this was not the way in corporates. In my first and second job I felt lucky to have this task done from my head office team as were mostly supposed to read and pitch what I used to ger as a content. The real problem started when I was in training job. Here I was supposed to make content on my own not only for my use but also for others to use and circulate. Thanks to my seniors in this job, I was used to read the product contracts daily and to make ppt on them on daily basis.

This rigorous task helped me a lot. From forty slides in starting I eventually reduced to twelve slides with same meaning to deliver! Now how I achieved this was by digging in five hundred meters into ppt. I learned effective use of all tabs in ppt. From slide colour, transition, animation pane, inserting objects, making videos etc. Even use of bullet points and later giving handouts alongside helped me reduced the size.

The most important point before making ppt was to understand who are your audience and their level of understanding and what was the message to be conveyed. This was something which provided a direction to select the style and animation types and content in ppt. Later I started making use of good videos and sound effects to give it a better feel.

10. Delivering Presentations – a good speaker

A good speaker is who listens to all. How a good presenter is who make audience mesmerised. No! you don't have to act like super star. The idea is to understand that you have to make the audience understand your points and message at the end of presentation. It's more about creating an aura and making the presentation lively and participating. This is the keyword.

How do we make it? I used to make a lot of blunders in beginning.

It was more because of lack of fear of public speaking. However, it vanished with time and practice. I first realised that I have to understand the purpose of presentation. Then knowing about numbers of participants and their background and the message to be delivered makes the task much effective. The venue and time allotted for presentation also made an impact.

Accordingly, I would decide my dress code, the banners and other materials. If the ppt was made by someone else then ensured to go through the same at least thrice or four times. If it was made by me, then use of bullet points was handy to make a crisp and clear presentation. I also developed myself on effective use of other aids like collar mike, projector and screen and pointer and slide changer. Even the use of "B" and "W" during presentation ensured that the audience was in sync with me.

Another important point I learned was that presentation slide is like your shadow. It must be in sync with your body movements and actions. It helps in creating a very effective impression. Further use of videos and sound effects and animations make the work easier. The presence of mind is much needed in presentations. It helps in quoting examples which are related and thus help in connecting with audience soon and deeply. Even being witty helps in achieving the task easily.

Most important thing which I learned was to speak French if people preferred French, no matter that I knew German as well. This meant to speak in language which the audience is comfortable. If the audience preferred Hindi or local language then I used that and If English or mix then I used to deliver the presentation accordingly. No matter who much I knew technical jargons and words or the quality of ppt, I always choose audience knowledge, participation and tolerance level above my knowledge and preparation.

Very importantly, don't lose patience in question and answer session. As there are hundred percent chances that there will be someone who would irritate not you know but whole audience with irrelevant comments and topics. Try giving relevant answers and close the presentation with a smart move. This is what I used to do mostly.

11. Telecall

This little tool of communication is good for making relations. I had tried making good friends online and there is success. People love the messages. I was also good at offline chatting with friends. But dear friends, talking to a friend is separate and calling on random number is separate.
It actually takes courage and confidence to call any random number and introduce oneself and try to convince the receiver for business. I do respect the patience level of tele callers and they deserve a standing ovation for not losing cool on the reactions received on calls. The rejection on call can still be handled. But when I had to call other numbers one by one and face rejections on few, then I realised the importance of word courage and confidence.

To sound cheerful on each call is a very tough job. Moreover, to win the trust of someone who has not seen you face to face and convince him for a business deal with you is really very different skill.
At first, I used to hate tele calling. But in sales one cannot ignore that. And that hold much importance when you are in business. I had to overcome this fear, which I did reluctantly. I started with first making three to four calls and then recording the feedback and this helped me in developing a small but effective pitch. It also helped in making good intro which is a good sign of pre sales.

The simple fact which can result in effective business is the list or database on which to call. This search for database led me to numerous lists of social clubs, companies list, religion list and so on. This list is never ending. I used to call on one list, scrap the negative ones and kept on adding new lists. Second factor is time to be given for each call. I experienced that if I made a pitch in advance and followed it, I was able to convey my points in lesser time. Only precaution was to avoid being monotones after few calls. I also ensured to not to call at odd hour. Now this is something subjective. People used to give me odd time to call back and I even don't know how many times I had to call for same thing. But this is part and parcel of this activity. I however made a point to note down remarks after each call. At least for interested call this made a good impression point as people would appreciate that I remembered and even recalled them about the previous discussion.

This experience also helped me in making impression and clearing junior expectation test, when I used to explode on them while doing tele call. The test which actually meant" *Sir, aap khud kar ke dikha do*" And clearing this test meant they won't challenge me and listen to me very carefully.

12. Door-to-Door

If I feared tele call then this was the worst nightmare I could have. The reason was obvious. This probably is considered one of the toughest activities you have to do in sales. Take my words, if you do it sincerely you will find yourself a changed person in terms of opening a conversation with others and also in getting mix up among strangers.

Words and motivation apart. This is tough means it is tough! I said this so many times to myself and to my seniors. The reasons were also supporting my fear. I used to call a random or known reference number to seek an appointment. Then I had to go there and wait at reception for a long time. This was somehow manageable and bearable as I had mobile to play games while waiting. And then the person meeting me after this wait and then his saying no or rejecting the proposals was a hell feeling.

Now I had a limited reference and these won't last forever. Hence the best way out was to generate own leads. So how did I did it? I first used to go to area survey. I used to prefer commercial area over residential. The purpose was to check what types of offices are there and the number of people working there and the type of people I would get. If the initial survey would pass the test then I used to check whether the area is suitable for my product to pitch. Thereafter I used to zero down on building whom I would visit on a day. Before the visit I used to prepare my war kit. It included enough no of visiting cards, my company brochure and any souvenir if I had the liberty to distribute them.

The next day, I would finish of office sales yoga and then have a little cheer up at the good" chai *ki tapri"*. Now you can do the call either way- start from upstairs or downstairs. The most irritating hurdles are two smart people. The security guard and if you cross him second is the reception front desk. Of course, this is their task to not allow any unwanted people in office. But here I used to apply the simple rule of good attire and minimal documents. Keeping a diary which had my few brochures and visiting card in hand, without any bag. This trick used to avoid the impression of salesman perception as viewed by many. However, the reception won't give you much detail so I used to try to get the office number and if I could get the person who can be first contact point then it was good. Repeating same thing floor to floor and office to office eventually would give few leads, few prospects and few negatives. Nevertheless, this hard work helped in controlling team when they would say that they are visiting this building and I could guide them or correct them or even teach them if they were going wrong with their purpose calls.

13. Head office meetings and corporate events

Many people like me would have been posted at branch office. For people serving at branch its mostly guest visit from above. There are very few who would be going to head office for good reasons. One such good reasons was head office meeting with seniors on targets and budgeting. Now this invite is like a needle hidden in chocolate. I too got such invite. Now here I was happy to visit head office and before that had to prepare for budget and targets and number of presentation and choose the content very carefully.

This practice is known as *"hara kiri"* in Japanese. Why I am using this term? Its because the budgeting and target meeting often results in accepting bigger targets than capacity. Even the company will freeze the same instantly. Avoiding the strong voice coming from head which is saying "No" on each target acceptance question with a fake smile on face and positive body language would have given me acting awards someday. But this is how this it works.

And at the end of the meeting they will usually keep an informal dinner with options of booze and merry dance. I would rather avoid getting too much indulged in this one-night stand. Usually the pinch of this is felt for long time in job. The reputation once spoiled is hard to regain.

Another important point which I observed and later always implemented was not to focus on choice of mode of transport and date of journey. This made me less targeted in terms of cost post meetings. Further a small trick which I used in hotel rooms before check in. I used to wait till end. This way I mostly used to get either a dumb partner in case of room share or mostly a single room.

Corporate events and fun events and parties are a common practice in big and mid-size companies. I used to be a spectator of preparations unless asked to contribute on preparation by my senior, I used to prefer written direction to save my neck later. One thing I observed was that these extracurricular activities is not going to add any relaxation in targets. Instead sometime this activeness resulted in increase of targets owing to ability to maintain high energy level at odd hours too. But in nut shell it's sometime good to be officially naughty.

14. Multi- tasking – a generalist will survive better

People go for specialization and even super specialization. I was neither of two. A plain graduate with few certifications. Initially I used to think about this a lot when I used to see my colleagues going better places. However lately I realised things don't work this way. In good times and in rising corporate revenue a super specialist will also get good growth however in times of slow down and cost cutting, it's usually them who are the first to leave. Rule is simple. In life one can afford luxury only in good times. Being a generalist was not a choice. But then this helped me having less ego in learning things. Hence, I was clear on one thing. Since I had no special skills, I cannot refuse learning additional. Eventually I could sell all category of products of BFSI industry and also understand the operational part of those. So, I made myself more saleable in job market. This multi-tasking which may be considered as a little importance thing in bigger companies, is seen as the biggest asset point in smaller or medium companies. In all situations, whether its growth or slag, I was able to justify cost and retain my job entitlement.

15. Not showing white flag – no surrender before searching options

This particular skill is in built in DNA of most of the persons. Usually people call such persons as Adamant. I too belonged to same category. This was first in DNA hence at student level this created in aggression. But in corporate I had to change. However, I made point to make it a positive change.

So, I used this skill to not to agree for any statement received for rejection by the respective back office team or any other associated company. This resulted in arguments first then me accepting their solutions to get the work done.

But the adamant attitude refused to just settle there. Hence whenever I got spare time, I used to look for possible alternative solutions to each issue I had faced. This led me to path of knowing the solutions from A to F and also the possible challenges, outcome and timelines of each solutions. This first became necessity then a habit. And it ensured that I was looking for possible solutions for each activity whether it was sales pitch, MIS, writing email reply, responding to client's queries and providing solutions and so on. In the process the mindset changed from being problem driven to solution driven. This actually helped me a lot as I was able to visualise possible hurdles in advance and be ready with alternatives. And because of this even juniors and seniors were ready to listen to me all times.

16. Logical – keeping mind open

There are few skills which one needs on daily basis to behave and act in front of many parties in corporate life. I could choose to be empathetic, rigid and logical at any point of time. Most of the colleagues I worked with were unwilling to even change or were very sincere for work rules. This statement can be read in many terms. Following work rules is must and good for company. But honestly, I have never seen company. All I have seen is people around me, driven by process with an ultimate aim of growth of both – themselves and the company they work for. The aim cannot be achieved with being rigid. Think of a case where you are working in a bank and have a good account which is held by a senior citizen. If there is any work in bank, he/she would have to come at bank on own or with some help. Then climbing stairs and coming at your desk. This is a tedious process for them. Still they managed and you see that they are failing short of a document. So, what you will do? This document requirement is such which can be skipped if you persuaded with your logical thoughts to yourself and your senior. Whether you will take pain for this persuasion upon yourself or tell them to come again with the documents. Other solutions can also be there. I always choose the first option. Call it nature or logically empathetic.

But the same cannot be thought in case of a client who required regular service. Otherwise each time I will be taking risk and one day it will eventually sink me. Understood the point? That's where I always insisted to use logic before action.

This I believe is the biggest challenge. I had seen people acting first and then thinking about the consequences. Maybe they believe in quote" *karam karo fal ki iccha mat karo*". In corporate life it's reverses. You need to visualise what fruits you will get otherwise you are looking for mangoes whereas your efforts are directed towards watermelons.

But as logical is good sometimes being rigid is the right strategy. Confused? I had faced situation where because of soft nature people will try to break the process too much or try to seek favours, high number of leaves etc and in process disturbing office code. Here the logical step was to be rigid and this is how I used to manage things around me. Logical in this sense will always mean being practical and putting mind before emotions.

This logical thinking also helped me in keeping my eyes and ear open to all possible solutions. At first, I used to get confuse and irritate when I had to pay attention to minute details to look for best first choice and hen alternative solutions. But as the time passed away, it became my habit to overlook the first gate in my front. And when I looked with open mind, sometimes I didn't have to walk towards door. My work was done sitting at chair itself. This was the pioneering skills which helped as booster for my career growth in terms of seniority and ability to handle varied task with resolution approach.

17. Pitch – how do you explain
I heard the word first during my sales training. It was a part of sales process and ensured that how would I introduce myself and company and products. Later when I became bit experienced, I

realised this word is applicable at all steps, whether its corporate life or personal.

In corporate it meant to know how to introduce juniors to clients, to introduce corporate and services and divisions to clients and so on. The correct word is how to describe and to ensure the recipient understands it. I practiced on pitch every day and to that extent that I could describe a product in one line and even for one hour. This development in pitch had an added advantage which I discovered later. I could speak on advantages as well as disadvantages of same product or service. Interesting, right? The advantage helped me to pitch my product and disadvantage helped me to counter competition product.

As per me an ideal pitch should speak about the inherent concept of the product straightforward. I recall telling a customer about systematic investment plan. As per me my pitch was" *Sir, any regular saving in instalments for a longer duration.*" Sometimes simple concept worked. But sometimes I had to use technical jargons if the other person was a knowledgeable person.

This pitch also helped me in giving or contributing in creative ideas for marketing materials like posters, flyers, etc. It made one liner effective to read and react upon.

18. Tech savvy

When I was a student and during my job I heard of programming languages like Java, C, C++, PHP, HTML, Python etc I also heard about Linux, Mac, Ubuntu and even terms like, networking, hardworking, wi-fi, connected device, Bluetooth printers, office network, security, licensed versions, anti-virus, database software, SQL Server, Cloud, remote application etc, etc. Some of my known persons were Computer Engineers, some did certifications from Microsoft and so on. They were expert in all these.

In today's time its funny that we have all technical devices which is mostly used by non-technical person like me and technical support is like calling to person sitting in Mars and speaking alien language. I am great fond of "*Ancient Aliens*" TV program but in reality, digging into details and banging head with technical person always resulted in a mess. I could have kept patience if this would have been a one-time affair. But I was dealing with these devices and systems on daily basis and couldn't rely upon them fully.

The option left was to dig a bit. Which I tried my level best. Reading through manuals and surfing through web and dear rescuers Google and You tube made me acquire a new term.' *Tech Savvy*'. This word meant in reality is that I could understand the pros and cons of each technology and technical device I was using. And also, was able to manage the basic functional hurdle on my own. This self – learning helped me in designing the office network when I was supposed to renovate the office and also helped in understanding the controlling factors and cost and risk of experiment involved in purchasing any device or going for any project.

And since in today's time most of the products are circling near and in distant touch with technology, this tech-savvy thing saved my life many times.

19. Rework

In my study tenure there was a quote which I can recall now" *Well Planned is Half done*" I didn't know the depth of quote then. Today at this stage I can safely say this quote is correct. I had done so many work and presentations and projects which actually turned up disaster in between. I will not say that the same was a failure however when you are involved with so many agencies and outside consultants or even internal teams, one or the other will ensure that the sorry tag in front of seniors is pasted on forehead for a good amount of time.

I analysed why such things happen? The major reason was not

having a complete blue print of the work. Many a times we rely upon words and forget that written is written and it needs to be honoured. I observed a good blue print included clear goals related to exact outcome needed, time lines, milestones, payment stages, type of agency required, material/service procurement, delivery required by all parties, remedial measures.

The problem which mostly lead to rework is failure to prove to the satisfaction. This word satisfaction is never achieved though. Every time I engaged my team for a project then everyone has different vision and thought. People even disagree on colour, layout, photographs leave apart content part. So, where does all this point? Not satisfied. Hence rework again till the rework person raises his hands up in air as this continuous rework is more work than original. Cost have doubled or even tripled. And then the work is stopped in mid. And all chaos.

To avoid all these, I tried to clear my points and my expectations from the agency. Also, I started to rely upon the agency for their part of expertise. And finally, I assumed and expected in beginning itself that the final outcome will never be as I though in my dreams. So better be happy with the reality and check on the progress so that its not that much deviated from what we thought.

20. Managing office events – clients and outside
Office events are moments of fun. Right? I must say its wrong. Actually, in such event I feel the pressure is very high as the expectations of the participants is quite high. It's fun for them. Client events and even distributor events or any other outside event is always a pressure. Participants expect great ambience, great food, great hospitality, great host and so on.

The things to manage are – venue, food, invite, decoration, goodie bag, presentation, arrangement for photo and video recording, sound system, host arrangement, registration, if any etc. etc. So, which to do first? The answer is All! You heard right. How can it be done, is a matter of skills?

The only task which can save the event day is team work. I did the same. I used to understand the tasks, plan a map in mind, call up various colleague's and divided the roles and work and ensured that everyone does the work including me.

The first step is to check for the kind of event and the approximate number of participants apart from the possible dates and time. Based on the info provided, the next step was to book venue. Now it's not just a phone. Sometimes the desired venue is booked for the day and the other venue is not so good. At other times the venue is available but the hall is an issue. Now I swear, I cannot imagine the hall just by hearing the fancy names as spelled by event managers. Best strategy is to go out and check the same in person. Once in person, I used to get surprises as somewhere parking will be an issue, and sometimes the hall placing would be odd as per the event required. The compromising situation is created thanks to the next-door hall which might have a birthday party and I was there to book a corporate conference event.

After crossing this another challenge was to scold myself for not doing a course in hotel management. Had I done that before, then I would have at least known what the dish will actually include and taste when I read the name of dishes as written in menu card. And then the task of finalising it. Whew! I had to check for non-veg, veg and some no onion no garlic dishes. Imagine my pain, as me having inclination for non-veg to always order for veg menu as in Central India most of the corporate preferred veg menu only.

The next step was to check for someone who has been a pass out of negotiation skills course. Reason was simple! The rates of hotels for venue and menu needed to be negotiated. With tax, without tax, minimum no of persons, additional items in menu etc needed to be discussed in fine details. This all exercise moved to a different direction in case I was lucky enough to manage a hundred percent sponsor or if there were multiple sponsors of the event. To give them due weightage during the event and to manage and sometimes suppress their expectations was a part of the management skill.

The first team will check for invitee list. If they have it then good, else prepare the same. This list needs to be checked with others and well to confirm whether the invitees are the same as desired and that no one must feel neglected. Remember marriage invite and some angry faces. Simultaneously, another person will prepare the invite. It will include small video, face book event, and online registration link. The invite must be as such that people feel interested in knowing more details which will prompt them to attend the session. In my career I experienced a strange anomaly in this registration. If it was a fee-based registration people are serious and will promptly provide all details and if its free session then the organisers has to follow for getting the details. Strange na! But this is what mostly happens. And therefore, the team had to follow up till the date of event to ensure attendance.

What to present in event and the content and host is another part. In big corporate events this task was allowed to be outsourced, of course under supervision. However, in small events it was about in-house preparations. In either of the case, use of proper language, videos, graphic effects, sound and flow of content was to be ensured as per expectations. This task became more difficult in cases when I had to arrange for presentations from various speakers and to create the flow and manage the distractions was a bit tiring task. Similarly, I would engage a team or be a part myself to arrange for goodie bags at or during the event and the handout and post event material distribution.

During the event the first point to check was the seating arrangement. Whether it was as per decided or not. I always ensured to reach venue at least an hour before. It gave me sufficient time to place all the promotional materials, check the registration desk. One important thing which I always experienced was during event either the sound or light system will always create a headache. Hence, I used to do a special check for same. Not for that the mess won't happen but that I had feeling that I checked that before.

I also ensured to engage few junior team or trainee in escorting guest to the seats, as this was a peculiar habit, I observed that people needed some additional magnetic force to be pointed towards the seats. Then the most important point to ensure was hosting. Whether we may be a multi-national corporate or an Indian one, the host experience has to be purely Indian, touching and caring like we all experience and expect in marriage.

During event serving of food or snacks is also a trick. If I used to serve them in hall then everyone will just concentrate their only. I also need to see my team as in our Indian tradition host always eats after all guests. So, I used to serve starters in between so that people can feed their light hungry stomach and concentrate on event. And then the next part was food. Mostly it used to be tasty but as expected in our marriages, here also I used to get comments on food and there were some very innocent people who will also find fault with few arrangements. Each such feedback found its place. Some min suggestion for next time and some in trash.

Post event goodie bags during event were mostly left by few participants. However, giving them in person and also possibility of giving them later in a gap of day or two, ensured a sift follow up with clients for the agenda of business.

21. Managing stock

Dealing in stock related business or serving companies dealing in physical stock proved to be a good experience. Thankfully I was not dealing with stock with expiry dates or out of fashion, so fast rotation was not pressure. However, the pressure in stock is there.

When I was in business, I used to have number of small items placed in shelfs and racks. To a client it's range of product, for me it was capital stuck in racks. Therefore, the pressure of monetising the stock fast was always there. In store I also learned the trick of placing stocks. The frustration was obvious. I n big stores we can use glass doors and fixed front glass wall. In small stores using this will keep client away as they might feel the high price shop feeling in their head. Therefore, dust was unwanted guest always. My staff used to clean the stock thrice a day. I also learned that clients won't be satisfied at any cost. They always wanted something new in spite of maintaining a good range of products. As if I was supposed to run a product laboratory rather than a store. A friend of mine guided me for this. He advised me to always change the position of stock every fortnight and to place the month-old stock in closed box and hen again take them out after a month. This actually worked for me. Of course, unless and until you have a regular customer who will figure out this trick after some time.

Another experience I had was of handling automobile stocks. Here I could not place it in another shelf as every model was different. Of course, I could play with colours of cars placed in showroom. But stock was stock. The pinch was the high cost of stock and the quantity of it. We had to have all colours, variants of all models of the manufacturer. It meant a huge inventory of vehicles, accessories and spare parts. This huge pile of inventory was subject to a test of one-year life as more the delay in date of manufacturing and date of sale, higher the discount that to be offered to any client. Further, the manufacturers upgrading or discontinuation of the models of the vehicle also had a negative impact on existing stock.

So, I used to place the showroom vehicle with accessories and also offered some paint customisations to offer uniqueness which helped me in getting fast orders of the vehicles. One thing which I learned in stock is that there is never a bad stock. We might think that the stock is stuck but somewhere out there, a client is made by God for that stock who will eventually come and ask for that stock. I remember the incidence when there was a special colour vehicle stuck in my inventory for long time apart from the fact that the manufacturer had stopped the production of that colour. I finally agreed to transfer that vehicle to another dealer at a loss. On the day when the driver of the vehicle was there from another dealer to pick the same, I suddenly got a client rushing in showroom and asking for that special colour only! And he took the vehicle at the price which I wanted with any other clients. See, somewhere someone is made for the stuck product too.

In case of stock which has varied prices, the stress is to clear the stock as soon as possible. Because the price will change on daily or weekly basis based on the market demands. The MRP is fixed but the profit margin changes. Hence need to draft the schemes carefully. Stock rotation was one such trick to use the last opportunity to extract maximum profit. It meant moving the stock from one showroom to another for some time specifically from stock of metro cities to be rotated In Tier II and Tier III cities. The last resort of course remains is sale.

In stock the other thing to remember is amount of discount offered to sell the stock and cost of various scheme which is done to promote product sales but eventually will be checked with actual no of sales. After facing initial challenges, I designed a layer of discount authority and also discount percentage for each level of my team. This ensured that each client feels he is being offered something extra. This strategy also ensured that I have varying profits for all vehicles but I could compensate the less discounted vehicles with high discounted ones and thus ensured that I had the average profit maintained.

During stock sales especially in case of finance facility the feature can turn into headache or in worst conditions a nightmare if the payment from the financer is not received in time or the case has been disapproved later. The challenge is to also sell and clear the stock and to maintain client ego as he wants the stock at the same moment and will use all powers and egoistic word to put an immense pressure on the sales person to go for delivery of the stock. This can be any product car, Television, mobiles, laptops etc. The range is enormous now. So, the smart tact is to have good relationship with finance company person as he is the one who can actually tell you the possibility of clearing the loan. In case of in-house finance, I ensured to have a good relationship with credit team not only for fast approvals but also to get clarity on proposals.

In stock one also has to face the challenge of return. This is more common in retail products more because of e-commerce. I would be happy in sales as my stock was cleared and also got accolades for that. And then the product returns may be due to some issue or client's personal conditions. Whatever the case may be, it's a double pain again. Not because I had the product back, it's because I already had the replaced stock to match the inventory and now this returned product. Now I would have pressure for selling two products. Next rule- never celebrate early in sales especially in stock sales.

22. Managing services

After going back to service industry from stock industry, I was happy as I won't have issues of stock. I will only have to manage my clients using my words and brain and that is an easy task. But soon this happiness faded as I failed to realise that in stock the client buys the product and the deals ends, the relationship ends whereas in services the relationship starts as soon as the sales is done and this relationship can go on for decades. In services industry the management jargon-*Customer Delight and Client Experience* were like twin swords which will have its impact on client feedback and finally client staying with the company.

In my entire career in service industry I came to few conclusions that in services industry there is no rule to judge why client would prefer me or oneself other person offering same services. Maybe he liked the pitch or dress up or whether he and me belong to same religion or region etc. I will not talk about company schemes and plans as they were same for everyone yet there were different sales figures of entire team. However, one thing is for sure. One can't see service but only feel it, therefore the sense of feeling of services and the expectation of treatment pre sales and post sales is always on a higher side.

Therefore, the word Customer Experience is a total experience of client from the day one I would approach hm for sale till the point of closure and till the time the client uses the services. This experience can be made good only with one view point in nutshell. The client will be demanding and in order to succeed I need to constantly upgrade in terms of knowledge and presentation and pitch. However, the pain is that the experience is a collective effort of entire team whereas the burden of experience is borne by the person who care about it voluntarily rest might just do their duties. Hence, what happened in real was that I used to end up losing clients because of the careless replies and approach of the operations and the support team. Now there are services where the client interaction is limited to on boarding only like selling SIM etc, In such cases the sales and services team are different yet because of the mistakes of the support team in handling the forms and not processing the requests on time, the sales person has to bear the grunt of the client even if he had sold him the services three months back. Similar is the case for support team when the client bangs upon them for the services and then they realise that the sales person has made extra commitments made due to lack of product knowledge or extra enthusiasm or target pressure. Whatever the reason be on both sides the client experience will take a hit and ultimately the client leaves the services.

In services where the relationships to be carried on on-going basis, by the interaction team only i.e. sales team handling and managing the relationship of client, the client experience management becomes more difficult. Usually for any good it was because of the client's decision and all bad was because of my decision. And here the issues came when I moved up the ladder. The clients whom I used to interact in my initial days of company would still call me up for all the petty issues and I had to ensure resolution as they were in touch with company and me since beginning. The issue was also mixed up when I had to meet clients who were older than me in the system and hence to make them understand my role and my position and then to win their trust on my capabilities was a herculean task. The picture turns into a horror movie with the demanding clients or clients who are much aware. At first, I used to listen them patiently to a stage where I started hating them and making a point to avoid the visit to them. However, I realised later that these clients are necessary in-service industry. If one is willing to grow then these are the best training grounds. In order to response to their queries on call and post the calls I had to prepare myself a lot with presence of mind and product and industry knowledge and also on paying attention and keen eye on minute details and fine prints. This made my approach more oriented on doing the work to closure at first instance and without much repetitions.

Client experience as per my understanding is nothing but taking care of client and his queries and timely response to calls and requests. It also means that whom so ever is the face of the company before client is knowledgeable enough to represent the company well. And more importantly the chain of the team which is handling the client is well connected and doesn't has any loop holes in communication. The best measure to have good sleep at night is to speak and commitment after thinking. Any lie to cover up will result in more layers of lie circled around a time bomb which will explode anyway.

As per my experience, Customer delight is a pro-active approach to ensure a good client experience. Written easily but very difficult to make as a process and follow the same. To be proactive you either should have a very sharp memory or a very dedicated team, which for me was not the ideal case. As I experienced it requires a team effort. As a senior I could only guide team, but if they didn't follow the process then the lacuna is immediately pointed out by the client. For a delightful experience I used to thanks to my tough clients who made my habit of paying attention to minute details and flaws. The most basic mistake which anyone makes in client servicing or sending any communication to client, is to check before sending. This simple task is most difficult to follow. We as humans are bound to overlook minute details and imagine my face as a senior when a client calls up and point out the silly and most usual mistake of error in name, address, phone number and email-id. For further enhancing the customer delight my company used loyalty points, rewards, events for awareness and entertainment, gifts etc.

All said and done, in my honest view the experience and delight is more based on paying attention to what client says and also what best can be done to close the task in minimum time with minimum hurdles.

23. Budgeting and planning

Thanks to all Tier II and Tier III B schools' advertisement on hoardings and posters and the speech given in these institutions, every would-be job aspirant in industry doesn't thinks below Manager or Associate Vice President level. Good! Thinking on positive terms however in reality the picture is different. I even had seen my few colleagues leaving job without proper financial planning and investing all the savings in just building the base foundation for the business. And then unfortunately the building is made on weak pillars which break off in a single blow.

To avoid such circumstances, I strongly believed in understanding proper budgeting and planning, esp. after my stint of business. I experienced that budget should be post planning. Yes, its true. Normally people take it to plan for the budget allotted. However, in real sense is to budget for the planned. This whole approach helps in keeping the feet firm on ground and ensures when we stumble or fall off, the impact and recovery is fast. In normal circumstances its' rising to sky through a plane and then to jump off from height only to find out the that either the parachute is not opening or even if it's opened, the wind has pushed the same in other direction and instead of landing at goal point, the landing is in deep jungle, hanging through a tree and waiting for help to come and rescue.

In corporates, the planning can be done for expenses. The income projections are different and are mostly a number gimmick and believe in God and praying to see God for taking his blessings. Expenses on the other hand, are a cruel reality and a situation when God sends an invitation to meet. To avoid this scenario the planning of expenses should be done in advance. The major planning is for important area like people recruitment, office area, office infrastructure etc. The routine expenses are vendor payment, distributor payments and general expenses.

Normally the difference between the budget then plan and plan then budget is the source of funds. If it's sourced through a source or backup or on loan then, since the pay-out pressure is not in present, the expenses are done via first approach. So typically, what happens in this situation is that we tend to burn cash. I did same too. The first lavish expenditure is in office or place, high rent, then good or very good interiors, then recruiting at least three to four persons team. All this done and then waiting for business from day one and each day. The happy cushioning soon sits down and what I realised that beneath that cushion it was a seat made of inverted nails. Now the pressure of rent, salary, EMI and other expenses came up. Forget what I was able to take home or even not take at all. The same happens in expansion mode also. I too was tempted with the taste of success in initial stage. And this boosted confidence to a high level. You can term it as over confidence. So, you might have heard of big showrooms closing their branches soon after launch or companies closing their branches after few months. This all is the result of jumping from plane.

The second approach of plan and budget is normally well when uses own resources and which might be a limited to some extent. So, the approach might give slow growth but then it will ensure that business is able to survive in rainy days and also is able to enjoy sunbath on beach when there is sun shine. My friends who used to follow this approach first invested in stock and distribution channel rather than big showroom and offices. Then the second investment was into small office and the third was in bank account to park the money saved. Their first motto was to build a steady cycle of sales and revenue and then go ahead for any investment in step up.

What I learned was the importance of most basic thing in corporate survival which I or most of the people overlooked and that is Cashflow. Whatever the excels tells or accounting knowledge tells. In reality its what I received in account post taxes and what I have to pay from my account. On top of it if I added expenses like fuel or time cost involved in follow up of revenue and creating that revenue then the net income will be more less. Even if the expenses are arranged through loan then the interest cost makes the expense dearer than what it was original.

So, the base rule is to understand that first build a base and then go for fancy things. But the question here is if everything is so clear in concept then why to plan budget. The simple answer is that it gives a picture of possible future and hence it gives a best view to plan for finances and cash flow in advance and that the image of a regular payment business has its own impact in getting good deals in terms of vendors and expenses.

My experience in budgeting, planning and understanding cash flow helped me in my corporate roles as well. The major planning in terms of three aspects of driving business like human resource, office infra etc were planed and executed with less experiment on cash.

Before starting any planning and discussion on budget the first important question which I used to ask myself was *"whether it's necessary and if yes then whether it's urgent? "If* the response to first part was *Yes* then, I used to go ahead with knowing the tentative cost and also used to do cost vs. benefit analysis. And if the answer to second question was also *Yes* then the budget will be decided accordingly.

For human resource planning, the biggest task it what number of team is required, then comes the expectation from the role and the experience required and then comes the cost to company. In planning process if feedback is taken from each then either you will end up with having no recruitment or having recruited an army. So, I used to filter the team required first by role expected and then the cost to company and importance of role, then I used to go looking for experience or fresher. In big company set up I could afford a stand by or alternative person in few months but in smaller companies the person has to be created with training on multi-tasking only. Another important point was to understand the growth of the proposed team in terms of role and package. Hence the planning which initially was for a year could also stretch for two or three years in case the candidate was good enough. However, I used to refrain from creating an army on the basis of business figures based on corporate logic. It meant that more the number of hands more the hands to feed. However, this octopus style wont work much as these artificial hands can't substitute the original hands for long. So, if I have to look for large number of team then I would also look for alternative of people on agency model and then to work out on projections for suitable model.

For office space my priority used to be to avoid luxurious and big offices at first. However again the same depends upon the team requirement. Bigger offices are mandatory when the team is large and in time of good business however in rainy days the rent will give a big jolt. Some might feel that the best is to buy out office when the company has funds. I am against this to an extent that in initial days, it's trial and error with locations and business, hence rented office is easy to vacate and relocate.

The office infrastructure is a very close to heart topic. People do expect the plushest office and equipped with all luxuries. However, I was of the view that if someone intends to work sincerely then the office infra is less important for him. So, for me I never thought on luxury. I applied this rule in spoke locations as well. I used to ensure that office can be small but it should look beautiful and importantly it should be functional.

This way I could control all expenses and ensure that the cash flow remains in control and that the cash crunch never hits the company.

24. Going Regional
In big corporates people are lucky to rise above a particular location and handle various locations. The same may be divided into spoke locations, area, region, zone etc. However, managing a branch is different than managing a whole area or multiple locations. I was one of the lucky ones to handle multiple locations in various roles.

When I was in agency channel, I had the team which was spread in three locations. The only difficult task was managing the travel as on few days I had to travel to two locations simultaneously. However, since the team was at par so management of team expectation across the locations was bit easy. The operational part however was to be taken care with patience as the form would take time to come and it might also require me to go to collect the forms in case of sudden urgency of business. Today thankfully we have good phone applications and software's and online mode to process the same across locations.

The situation changed when I was promoted in my second job, Here I was heading on role team spread in various locations. Now here the challenges were to identify the grapevine network, ensure that there is no favours to anyone. Even the branch cost would be added to my area cost an di was responsible to justify the same. And the best part was that since each member had different mindset and personality and attitude, to align their focus and to keep them moving ahead in single direction was the task which was new to me. Sometimes I failed to understand why the result varies in all locations in spite of having good strategies in place for directions. Then I decided to roll the sleeves up and check out myself. The first step to take in this case is to double the tour days. If going for one day then go for two days. Normally in a single day tour the productive hours to meet and understand the team and the clients or other issues is difficult. Next before going, try to identify big names of the industry or clients or famous business locations so that one can check the economic strength of the location and see whether the team works in proper direction or not. Once in location the best strategy is to reach before office opening. It also gives a check on few disciplinary issues. During the visit I used to ensure to travel the location by all descent modes, car, two- wheeler or even by foot to understand the market distance and in this way, I used to get a fair idea of geographical and business mapping. Post visit, I used to ensure to keep in touch with few clients and team members and also with the agency channel, if in the system, to ensure getting the information about working and also in gathering information about competition.

This strategy works well in case when the area is direct under supervision. However, when the area is handled by respective branch heads then the situation is different. I used to follow all above steps and also used to do branch head meeting on strategy and targets. So, in this case the additional layer of meeting is of branch heads meeting. The main agenda of course remains to discuss the targets. I used to prepare myself with MIS data in advance so that I can always check on the reality and do not rely on assumptions. Another important point for discussion in the meetings will be costing and any client issues. Costing is very important to control as the slippage result in getting the issue high-lighted in my meeting with my seniors and I definitely wouldn't want to have sorry face in meetings. The main expenses in branch are tea and snacks, courier and travel expenses of the team. It should justify the business done and revenue achieved.

As a location head, one has also to ensure that the team remains happy with support from upside. So I used to forwards the travel bills for further clearance in time and also used to help with team by giving them few references for business from time-to-time. One also has to be patient in listening to team's query and challenges. The major reason is that the middle management or location head is a sandwiched position between top management and lower team. And to strike a proper balance in the skills required.

25. Understanding all specializations – finance, operations, HR, marketing, admin, housekeeping

In job, I used to think that being a MBA makes difference in job. Yes, it does makes difference in packages in many companies. However, the skills make the bigger difference later. Being an MBA is not the guarantee of success. However, acquiring MBA skills is surely the passport to success trip.

The skills are the specializations which any management student will learn every six months during his semesters. These are finance, operations, human resource, marketing, and operations. The application in corporate life is different. Now people may argue why to learn all skills if we have taken specialization in one stream. The reason is based on experience. All the skills are inter-related. How? Have you ever heard any HR manager or sales manager who doesn't wants salary? Similarly, I have never seen a sales manager who has not to deal with team. And very few people are there in organisation who don't have to work as for working you need to have operation skills so as to complete the work in time. This skill set is necessary if someone ever wish to rise in job to a good position and even wants to do self-job. Only the approach will change which eventually meet at the top level in job as one cannot survive in top position without having the business approach.

The finance skills and core understanding of concept, help in knowing the real return and cost vs benefit. The best teaching, I learned from this skill is that there is cost involved in each step. Whether we consider it or overlook it, is subjective. Considering the cost makes the habit of looking for options for each decision. And in turn it helps in making the image of cost justifier. In other sense, every business goal and job goal are eventually connected with money and hence one cannot ignore the importance. So, I focused on this skill as a part of keeping people happy in terms of the most basic expectation. In job I used to ensure that the team gets their incentive timely as per policy and also that their costs are justified with proper actions. And not only team but my distributors should also get their pay-outs on time. I also was able to design and implement incentive cycles to keep every participant of the business food chain satisfied. In business recovery time, this helped me making proper planning of cash flow cycle so that I can get the desired image of good business practice and enjoy discounts on this practice. And trust me, if the cash flows and money is dealt well, the business or company as the case may be, always gets good people who wish to do business with you or good people who wish to join you.

The finance skills understanding also helped me having an alignment with company goals. I have experienced that someone who understand the same and even acts accordingly is normally having the most secure and long-term stint in any corporation. This applies to even people who take project jobs and in IT sector. As I have seen many people failing to understand the cost involved, hence quoting wrong costs to clients. And when the reality of deficit comes in, then either the works quality is deteriorated or the team is sacked for mitigating expenses. This in final outcome results in shifting of clients to other.

The next important skill to understand and practice is human resource. Now how does it touch all. I am not saying of dealing with colleagues. I am more focused on dealing with team on job and other models which used to report to me. The worst part I have seen is bosses and seniors failing to understand this simple point. I have claimed that as senior one must be tough, but then coconut is also tough from outside but inside its soft. So, taking this example I used to practise toughness in goals and dealing with clients, flexibility in actions and was soft in understanding the problem and providing solutions. This habit of providing solution ensured that my team was relaxed at back of the mind that I will always save them whenever they land in deep trouble or need immediate SOS. Remember, a good boss is not who can pin point the issues but the one who can provide the solution to resolve the issue. I followed resolution approach. This in turn made them satisfied with work and hence they were able to provide best services to clients and also were ready to work for long hours in case the task demanded so. Of course, this approach led to nuisance also as some people used to take liberty of this nature but soon, they were not my team so I used to focus on productive team only. Another advantage was I used to share professionally good and personally empathetic relations with team. So, even if they switched role or location in same company or other, they will stay in touch with me. Think that if I have to work with them again then this nature ensured they will jell up with me again. It also helped me in getting my work done fast as I could always depend on them in case, I needed their reference for a work of mine or my present company or for anyone else in need.

The next important skill to practice and implement is operations. It simply means knowing the process and how the products or services are delivered to clients and also how does the company realises the payment for the supplies done. To deliver the commitment or over commitment made in sales the backend team works hard to ensure that the client remains with company.

But it's the task of backend team and why should someone in sales be worried about it. Right? To some extent yes. But if someone wish to be to a true successful boss then knowing operation is must. Even in my career, Once I started paying attention to operations, I was able to serve the client well. I knew in advance what the client will expect hence I used to build my process around that and then used to commit in sales accordingly. It helped in saving me from hassles of managing lies and trying to hold on client. Instead I had satisfied clients who knew that my commitment will be full filled. Next important thing was once I knew operations at back end then I was able to align all activities internally in harmony with other departments. This also ensured that I was able to realise the payment from clients in case of credit on time as the process was well cleared to them and my team as well. Hence the both sides were happy most of the time.

Apart from these basic skills one must also know the admin skills. This looks awkward as this is the task of admin person but then think of a case when you decide to have your own set up. Then who will do it? So, to avoid this and have a pleasant experience ensure that at least you know the number of agencies or contact person who can be called upon in times of emergency and routine inspection of assets. This ensures that the work is not suffered due to poor infrastructure and also that the client experience while visiting the office is very good.

All said above most of the people look marketing as very tough skill and that is the part of head office person. But they fail to realise that each one in company is doing marketing and is responsible for this. The concept is simple. Everyone is a brand ambassador of family image in front of other. The same applies to company job. I realised it in early jobs that avoiding this means creating toughness for self in future. So, I used to pay much attention to company dress code, process laid, my behaviour with clients and distributors, even when I was going on travel then during travel and during stay. This all ensured that I created a good image for my company which in turn will help me or someone else in my company. Me most as if everyone does the marketing job properly then its an experience for others and then this helps in enhancing my image that I work in this company. See, the result. Its boom rang effect. So you saw so you reap.

26. Clarity in goals and business models

Written easily but learned in hard way. The clarity is at most important If someone wishes to avoid the term experience in negative sense and also to avoid rework. I am of firm view of this clarity. It helps in knowing the clear expectations and the strength and limitation of resources. It helped me in one way. That I was firm on my actions as I knew where I wanted to head in terms of achieving goals as laid down by company. This in real term helped me in satisfactorily handling the expectations of team and company and clients and hence led to fewer frowned and sorry faces. So, I used to tell the team clearly about the goals, the actions required to achieve it and the bottom lines of tolerance and integrity. For me any deviation meant giving one more chance and in case of repetition the member was no more a part of team. For clients the clarity meant what they expected from me and company when they are buying the product or using the services. This gave me an opportunity to say no to a client if the expectation was far from reality or such which was beyond my authority to commit. This also ensured aligning my backend so that the client experienced exactly or closely to the expectation set in meeting. With my seniors the clarity was much needed in terms of their expectation out of me and my team. This I think is of most importance. Any doubt in actions and methods on both sides results in first dissatisfaction and then disassociation. And since the boss always sit above, the chances of me getting hit by his bullets were higher. And I didn't want that. On companies side the clarity is required to understand internally where the organisation is heading in terms of immediate and long-term priority as after all my career was also mixed with it. Externally clarity is required how to deal with the associate vendors and distribution team so that they are also able to deliver as expected.

The clarity on what business model to adopt also gives a clear indication of the result to be expected. Of course, in long term the strategies can be changed for better survival. However, the frequent changes can always hamper the image. The models can be online or physical, agency model or own team, single location or multi location, single product or multi products, sales oriented or customer services oriented. Each type of business model has its own different impact in terms of costing, gross and net revenue and the time required to achieve the goals. Even the contingency plan will differ for each model. Which is the best model being the question of long debate. Better suited to own desire and capacity and willingness to taking risk in terms of capital and time involved alongside availability of quality and number of resources.

27. Entrepreneurship and job mentality

A very personal topic. But worth mentioning here because as per me it's the base of growth in job. I too rose may be due to this. Hope so. The difference is simple and obvious. A job mentality means that I am concerned with my salary date, my job location, my transfer, my travels expenses, my targets for the year, my grade in job, my expected hike in salary and role, my incentives rate, my working hours. And I will less care about costs, profit of company, client retention, other ancillary costs. And on top of it what my colleagues are getting. Keeps me happy and focused on my satisfaction.

On the other hand the entrepreneurship mentality meant I will focus on long term costs and benefits, what I am actually able to generate for the company, what best I am doing to promote all products and other head of company, my responsibility on my commitments, what type of resources I am able to develop for my company and that what I deserve in the end if I play my part well. As per my experience one can definitely survive through job mentality but I have seen great CEO's only when they were able to turn and tune themselves to entrepreneur mentality.

28. Handling People
Your boss

The word spikes many thoughts in the mind. There are many quotes on all channels of wisdom on boss and their qualities and attitudes and so on. However, remember the golden fact – in life, there are two very important persons, father and boss. Unfortunately, you can't choose who the same will be. And they both can either make your life or ensure its screwed like hell. So, be patient and tactful.

All this based on my experience as junior and boss both. In job either you will get a good boss or a bad boss. Tough, disciplined, strict are other attributes which can be present in both types. A bad boss typically will try to harass you in person and public as well. And will also scold you day and night on all reporting groups. You will also feel the burden of target to the level of stress. Forget about the support. You might also see favours for others. Few of these go to extent of even giving negative feedbacks in performance reports and even in feedback calls from new employers.

In contrast a good boss will try to council you in terms of performance and will also support team. He might also be able to give you solutions and will stand in terms of team support. The praise in public will come hand in hand apart from being concerned with your development in terms of personal skill and in job.

However, before making a final verdict on boss my suggestion is to wait and see. I too had gone through this dilemma. There can be instances that it was my mistakes which prompted boss to immediately behave in that manner. Or it may be that he too is stressed and pressurized from top management. But however, if the ragging continues for some time and the support side is lacking then one need to think and act smartly and try to figure out for a solution on priority basis. Don't look for strategy like becoming a devotee or surrendering to his terms so as to win his confidence and survive. If the person was good enough, such situation would not have arisen at all. Even leaving job in frustration or fear will not help. As in such haste you will not negotiate well and you never know you might get the boss of same nature again. See from fire to frying pan.

However, a good boss can be negative in long run. His always supportive nature will not let you grow as you will develop the habit of living in a protected cocoon. A happy boss will make you lazier and less confident on self. Sometimes too much sugar also creates issues.

I used to pray for getting a rational boss rather than either of both sides. A rational boss can be tough and strict but I was sure that in terms of support he will help out when my all strength has gone or when I am cornered with having little chance to escape. The rational boss will also help in developing myself by allowing me to take self-decisions and also allowing for a chance to make mistakes and rectify the same. May all get boss like this.

However, if someone is willing to finally get into business, then the best quote to follow is" *if you wish to be a lion, then train yourself with lions*" So, the small companies are a good way to learn and train yourself only if you are willing to be loyal to firm till you start your own. The negative side is that since the organisation is small then all the heat from promoter/owner comes to you and also that all activities which are done are either routed through you or affects you. However, the positive side is that the learning is very fast and accurate.

Your colleagues
Just like in family you can't choose your brothers and sisters similarly you can't choose your colleagues. So, what you can do is

simple thing which I used to do when I used to get frustrated with them *"Control …control"*

The best way to deal with the colleagues is to be professional and not emotional. How I work in reality is case to case basis. What happens is that we work with colleagues at least close to eight to ten hours on daily basis. Even some might live in same campus or near by location. So, the warmth in relationship is sure to happen and hence the border line between personal and professional becomes thin. The fun part is that now there are new corporate cum personal friends to work with. The negative aspect is the seriousness in roles gets faded away and is felt more if there is a change in role putting you or the other in senior position.

Another point is that you may be working too seriously and your counter parts or other department people are fun living or viceversa. In corporate life, the magnet works opposite. Here the same side attracts and different sides pushes in other direction. In corporate life the point is of team spirit. And as you know no one has ever seen spirit in real life, hence this dear team spirit always lies deep inside the flesh of targets, competition, jealousy etc. So, I used to refrain from getting too much personal with colleagues. Some might have called me rude or egoistic or otherwise. But I felt that the behaviour was necessary to avoid unnecessary emotion in working and that I could also get authoritative as and when situation demanded. It doesn't mean that I didn't made good corporate friends. I made them in each company but restrained from getting personal. And till today I share very good professional relationships with them.

Similar like boss, the colleagues can be good or bad or neutral or dead weight. Here the point is different. The bad colleagues make you more alert and also frustrated mostly. The gentlemen or otherwise, will be busy in pointing your mistakes to your senior or to even you team. Will always invent ways to ensure either you are down in system or even leave the system. Dealing with them is such a fun in positive ways only if you know your moves better in advance. Whenever you need to reply them, the best strategy is to check your defence system as the bombs can be thrown from any side. The worst such persons can say in case of help is *"I don't know how to do it"* even though they might have doing the same for last five years. Thanks to this approach, I made myself better by training on own hence the dependency on others became less and less.

The good colleague is one which will support you from back and also will listen to you and will be a partner with you at famous office stress escape points like cafeteria or the humble tea stall. The gentleman will also ensure that you know of the boss is there in office when you are outside for a personal work. Happens sometimes! The best part of having such colleagues is that going to office is fun and that you know that you might not carry stress back at home. The negative side is that if the person leaves the organisation then there is an impact in working harmony which gets disturbed for some time. The neutral colleagues are good for office parties and singing birthday corals whenever required. They are the person who reminded me that office timings are actual in practice at office. Else for me office timing was only on offer letter. The neutral colleagues are good for supporting the office system and in making you have the feel of four-hundred-meter hurdle race in case of emergency. The most dangerous type of colleagues is that who will always lean upon you for support in office politics and work issues. I prefer calling them dead weight. This type is typically doing job because of some pressure from home or is always pressed in family matters. The office pressure is also felt most by them. So, what they do is to lean on a person who gives them support and guides them. And once done is to be done always. Hence the work used to suffer. The biggest pain was that the gentleman was never willing to upgrade. He will simply rely for each matter and this creates double frustration in job, one of own and other of his. So better to stop the practice sooner or later.

You junior-

The junior team is a cute gift mostly. Either they will be like small kids. No matter how much you train them they will always work in their own manner which involves lots of mistake coupled with over commitments. Or they will be like trained autoboots. Will work as per feeder data only and will lack use of self-brain.

However, they are very important part of corporate chain. Without them the upper staff can't be productive. They are the actual persons who are the face of company in front of clients. Hence the need of training and discipline and motivation is must. At this level the major challenge is to ensure less attrition. The juniors tend to switch job very frequently. So, strategy like parties, gifts, incentives etc is the best recourse to sustain the team.

The above is good thing in case of freshers and base level junior team. But if someone is lucky to have junior at just one or two level below the self-grade then the situation is different. The immediate junior has to be handled like care. Else the same will prove like headache. The best moral I learned is that, in order to grow one must teach and develop the juniors to take better positions. This will ensure that my position is elevated for bigger roles. However, the same is to applied with precaution. Else the junior at low pay scale with kind of your knowledge is a better option for companies.

In business the things do change. When you are accustomed of having an army of juniors, it's difficult to survive without the aura in business. Here the juniors are profit eaters in beginning. So, the temptation to hire number of juniors should be kept in control till there is enough revenue and return to justify the cost.

29. Reporting

This word is very simple to understand. People fear it most and try to manipulate it. The base rule is- *"can you imagine your body with water?"* No. Right? *Similarity no corporate can't be imagined without reporting.* To try to escape from it like running in ava-lanche. It will take you over eventually.

As a junior I too used to hate reporting. But then I realised its going to stay and I have to change. Though the reporting formats and numbers changed from company to company. Somewhere it was excel, concalls, video calls apart from individual calls and feedback. In newer age the new weapons of reporting are whats-app and other applications. The essence and meaning are same. One very important thing I learned as a junior. Prepare the MIS on time and keep the reports ready else the pile up will ensure that the same is being told to clean up on odd hours or in case of ur-gency which will lead doing the things on gun point.

Once was promoted, I had a different view of MIS. I was wrong in saying it a s a burden in my initial days of job. Imagine you are not in the location and want to see the progress or status of work. So, what will you do? Will you call each one in person and then check or will make visit too often? Both are practically impos-sible. Here the reporting comes in handy tool so that the clear and crisp picture is presented so that same can be analysed and pre-sented to upper management. An experienced senior can always vouch this that this simple and humble MIS is never ready on time and in case of emergency, it's the senior facing the brunt. A small tip for getting exact MIS or reporting is to check the report and comment randomly. It will ensure the impression that the MIS is being checked daily and minutely hence the deviation from ac-tual will be very less.

30. Observation

In my entire career I have learned one thing- that learning is diffi-cult. No one want to teach you. Further the lack of base skills education and difficulty of getting formal education for each skill make the task much tedious. To keep the willingness and enthu-siasm open for learning new things is not possible when one has so much negativity and le pulling and stress in corporate life. Its very easy to just download the software update for any device but there is no such skill update for human beings. So, the best use of human sense like eyes and ears is to be done to use the best strategy to learn continuously. That's observing. *Yes! I am right.* This word means observing the environment and people around you and try to learn how to react in each situation. Formal skills do help but the informal skills save life. Hence the best method is to become respected *Eklavya* and do the self-learning by observing. Though a humble advice is to not to tell anyone about the teacher as it will result in loss of ability to show the skills. Its, Corporate dear! Hence the survival rules are different. And based on the skills and observing and practicing them one can surely Evolve from situation where he says yes Sir to a situation where other say him yes Sir.

Part 4

Corporate tales from here and there

1. Sailor and intelligent scholar

One day a man, who was very scholarly, was returning from the city and he wanted to cross a river. He found a boatman nearby. He said to boatman: hey boatman, will you take me to the other side of river to my village?

Boatman said: yeah sure, i am waiting here for taking passengers to the other side only.

The scholar gets into the boat and boatman starts rowing the boat.

The scholar was very happy to return to his village after a long time and started talking with the boatman.

Scholar said: Boatman, do you know what Ms-Word is, how mail merge works?

Boatman: no sir, I just row this boat across the river.

They proceed for a few moments.

Scholar said: Your life is 25% wasted. You don't know anything.

Scholar asked: Do you know about PowerPoint; do you know animation and slide design and charts to display forecast?

Boatman said: i am an illiterate man, I dint understand a word what u asked.

Scholar said: oh 50% of your life is wasted.

Scholar: you know advanced excel. With all data coming over us, do you have any idea what a graph of probability would look like?

Boatman: i don't know sir, i just row this boat.

Scholar: ohh, 75% of your life wasted.

Then all of a sudden there was a cloud, a black dense cloud on the sky, and there was a storm.

Boatman: sir, do you know swimming?

Scholar: no i don't.

Boatman jumped into the river to save his life.

Boatman: then you have lost 100% of your life; you are going to be drowned.

Moral: Whatever else we may learn in our life's journey, there is one thing we all need to know: how to cross safely to the corporate world when its time of storm.

2. King and Minister

Once there was a king who had four ferocious dogs. Whenever he would become angry with anyone, he would throw the person in front of the dogs and they would tear the poor man into pieces in no time. Everyone in the kingdom used to fear and would pray for not doing any such mistake which led them to this punishment. One day unfortunately, the prime minister of the King, committed a mistake and was announced the punishment. Now the minister pleaded, *"Sir, I have served you for ten years, can you please forgive me or just allow me one-month time to serve the punishment?"* The King refused for forgiveness and allowed for one-month time. The minister straight forward went to the dog keeper and told that he will serve the dogs for next one month.

The minister would take care of bathing of dogs, would

feed them well and also would take care of them for their exercise and will play with them. On the date of punishment, a large crowd was gathered in the arena to watch the fate of minister. He was called upon and the four dogs were brought in arena. The dogs were left open. And they pounced towards minister. To everyone's surprise the dogs started wagging their tales and started licking his feet and sit by his side. The amused King asked the minister for this behaviour of dogs. The minister replied *"Sir, this is returning of love. I served them for just one month and they returned love instead of death to me and I had served you for ten years, yet you are not ready to forgive me for a small mistake"* The King was silenced for few moments and looking towards his minister ordered his guards to fetch the minister to crocodiles!

Moral of the story: If the management has decided to screw you, then they will do at any cost.

3. Presentation by Mulla Nasruddin

Once Mulla Nasruddin was invited to give a presentation to an important gathering of students. He enthusiastically prepared the presentation and was at the presentation hall on time to deliver the same. Post his three-hour presentation he reached home and his wife asked *"How was your presentation?"* To which Mulla Nasruddin replied *"Which presentation? The one I prepared or the one which I gave or the one which I now think I should have given?"*

Moral – Whatever you plan, things will always be different while delivery

4. Lion and Jackal A boss is friendly not a friend – handling team

Once in jungle, there was once a very powerful lion. Everyone in the entire jungle was fearful of him. One day he unfortunately was trapped in a swamp and shouted for help. Luckily a jackal was passing by. He saw the lion and immediately through a branch which Lion caught from other side and jackal managed to pull him from swamp. From that day the jackal used to eat free food from Lion and also started participating in kingdom decisions. Other members of council were jealous of the same. They warned lion about the jackal and his casual approach. The Lion noticed the same. One day jackal in a normal mood mocked kind in front of his counsels. The Lion got angry and raised from his seat and jumped in front of jackal and tore him to pieces.

Moral – Always remember, a good boss is friendly but not a friend.

5. Fox and Elephant

Once in a jungle, a fox opened a bakery shop. And since there were not many shops in that jungle, it flourished well in less time. The clients would visit the store in person and sometimes will also wait to get their product. Upon seeing this good response, one consultant suggested him to go for online booking of cakes which will save the clients time. The idea struck fox and he also started taking online orders.

At one such festive day he got an online order from Mr. Sumo, a known business man and big elephant in size. Unfortunately, due to rush, the fox forgot to check the online orders and just as his sixth sense gave a ring, he checked the online and was just about to faint as the order was already placed four hours before and the client would reach the store in another half an hour. Now the fox was doomed. He needed at least an hour and half to make the cake and deliver the same.

But then his service industry friend dropped in and listening to this situation and checking in the online order suggested a solution. The fox immediately set in work to prepare the cake and till the time the client reached the store the cake was ready for decoration. The client asked about the cake and the fox replied that unfortunately the client had failed to click the topping on cake. And since it was an important event, he couldn't risk putting just any topping. The client was taken aback for a moment but then the fox face was so innocent that he relied upon him and asked for the suggestions. The fox was quick to suggest and also to commit of home delivery within an hour so that the client can do another work till the cake was delivered. Fortunately for all the cake was ready and was delivered in forty-five minutes just in time. And the elephant was happy with the cake topping and the services.

Moral – In client servicing either commitment or candy works to save the life.

6. Father and Son

Once in a small town there lived a small businessman who used to get just enough to manage the earnings. One day he was travelling with his son to a near by market. On the way they found a person selling an elephant. The boy started to push his father for buying the same. The father was reluctant and told son to go and check out for pricing. The boy went to find out and came back and said, *"We can buy the same at 1 Rs"*. To this father replied *"Let be! It's expensive."* And they continued their journey.

Few years passed by. Meanwhile the business flourished good. One fine day the father and son both were going to market and they saw a man selling an elephant. The son remembered his childhood and asked father *"if we can buy the same."*. The father sends the son to check the price. He checked and came back and said *"We can buy the same at 1000 Rs"*. To this father replied *"Buy it! It's cheap."*

Moral – Always look for your budget and cash flow. Sometimes a cheap deal is expensive and at other times the costly things are cheap.

7. Lawyer and Witness

Once in a court room during a trial the lawyer was cross examining a murder witness. On each instance the lawyer will say to witness *"you have said this, hence we can assume…"*. This being said many times on each statement said by witness. Finally, the witness got irritated and said "Sir, every time it's not possible to use direct logic" The lawyer got annoyed and said *"It's not possible. You can ask any question and I will prove that direct logic exists"* The witness asked" *Sir, if you are able to see one km from one eye, then how far you will be able to see with two eyes?"*

Moral – In corporate life, it's better to be practical than logical.

8. King and Saint – tension in managing kingdom – job and business

Once there was a king of a large kingdom. He was always busy and won't even find time to enjoy with his family. Once his Guru, a renowned saint, paid visit to him. He saw the king so busy and thus asked, what's the issue he is facing? The king said, *"O holy one! I am so tensed in my daily life. Every day I wake up I have to meet the various people who would come with all sorts of complaints. Then I* also have to meet with my council and see their workings. I always fear for their intentions if they are loyal to me and are not trying to kill me. I also feel tension due to the surrounding kingdoms if they are not planning to attack me and kill me and take away my treasure. Therefore, I have kept many guards in treasury to watch but still pay a round daily to see if things are proper. This has made my daily life so unrestful that I am not even able to sleep"

The saint said *"Don't worry my child! There are solutions to each problem. For this you can handover your kingdom to me and can rule the country on my behalf till I am out. I will pay our visits in between to check if things are working fine"* Now the King used to respect his Guru so much, so he agreed to his solution and handed over the kingdom to his Guru. And started ruling the kingdom in his behalf.

After some time, the Guru paid a visit to meet the King. The King was much happy this time and was looking relaxed. The guru asked the reason for him to be happy. The King replied *"O holy one! The day you have taken the kingdom, I am so relaxed. I now get up on time and listen to the people with a solution to be provided by council. I also do not fear the council anymore for their loyalty and even the treasury guards. I realised that I am being paid well for my services and that since the entire kingdom is your then its your tension, not mine!"*

Moral – There is a difference between the job and business mentality.

9. King and Guards

Once there was a very kind hearted King ruling a small but flourishing kingdom. He was very people centred and soft hearted. He would ensure his guards and council always work in best conditions. So, he decided to have made policies for using the best chariot for travel and to spend a good amount while travelling with all allowances allowed. He would also pay for the medical assistance for guards and their families.

For his guards and council, he also made a very plush council room and guard room where they can work. The air will also be filtered with perfumes and all sorts of scents. But one fine day, he got a letter from his guards, that they are not happy with the quality of scent used in rooms and hence will do a boycott of work, if the solution is not provided.

Moral – In companies most of the people fail to understand the difference between rights and facilities and therefore remain dis satisfied and a pain for system in whole.

10. King and The Warrior Saint

Once there was a king who was fond of hunting and also paying visits to his kingdom subjects in disguise of an ordinary man. One night while he was roaming, he forgot the way and took another path. Walking for a long time, thirsty and tired he saw light coming from a small hut in distance. He rushed in there and asked for some water. The hut belonged to a saint who helped King regain his energy and offered water and some food. After some time, the saint was ready for his night walk and King was surprised to know that the saint was going for hunting. Curiously King asked to saint that if he can accompany the him. The saint nodded in positive.

They both left the hut and began walking towards town. On the way they found a group of people discussing about the share in earning. They hid in bushes and king was surprised to see his fort guards discussing about the sharing in income which they will be getting from another king if they allowed the entry. The king become so angry at those traitors that he wanted to kill them at once but the saint stopped him and told to continue the journey.

While they continued, they heard voice of music and clapping. The king saw a very smart man wearing white clothes enjoying the dance of very beautiful dancers and drinking wine. His disciples were sitting below to him and they too wee enjoying. Then the saint told that the person is a very holy man and in day light wont even touch the material things and talk about simple life. The King became curious and wanted to continue the journey. The saint took him to next stop where the King heard a man asking for money for clearing the bills of another person. He recognised the person who was asking the money was his treasurer. Upon seeing all these the saint told king *"A king should always visit his kingdom and hunt for these types of people as these are the people who bring corruption in system and also are responsible for the weak system and values and must appreciate and reward the person who he founds to be kind and loyal"*

Moral- A head of department responsible for an area or region must be alert and also must pay visits regularly to check if there is all good in company.

11. The Traveller

Once there was a business man who was travelling in an economy class on an airplane. He saw the passenger next to him was busy reading some documents on his tablet. Since the journey was of three hours, he started conversation with the person. He was surprised to see that the person sitting next to him was the CEO of a very big company and was going to attend a conference. The first gentleman was also going to attend the same conference as a distributor of the company. He asked to the CEO *"Why are you travelling in an economy class, when you can afford a charter flight?".* The CEO smiled and said," *I knew about this travel plan in advance and that the event is just a formality for me and a cost expense for company, so I thought that my travelling though business class for such a short trip won't add sense to the costs. However, post this conference I am going to meet a client, who is supposed to give a very big order and therefore I have booked a chartered flight since my client is available for a very limited time and I don't want to take chance on regular flying times"*

Moral – In business one must know the purpose of costs and what is urgent and important. Sometimes even Hundred Rupee

is important and sometimes even One Lac is waste and vice versa.

12. Two Prince

Once a king had two sons. He used to be in dilemma as to whom he would see as a king in coming times and whether the people will approve. He discussed the same with his chief minister and he suggested a solution. Both the princes were called upon and were given the task of making a bridge across the river in one month. They were given the required tools, machines and a team of contractors, labours and consultant to finish the task.

The king was happy to see both the team working and in bridge work in progress. On the day of the bridge opening, he was welcomed and greeted by a large crowd. He saw both bridges and appreciated the team. Then he along with his chief minister and other people decided to take a ride on both. He first walked to the bridge made by his elder son. The bridge was simple built and also had strength to get the chariot cross it without any hurdles. The bridge also was able to stand in times of high tide. The king crossed the river and in return choose to ride through the bridge made by younger prince. As soon the chariot was in between, the bridge started shaking and before the king could cross it completely, the bridge fell off. The king and his subjects somehow managed to survive the fall.

The king called both princes and asked the younger one first how did he made his bridge? The prince replied *"I didn't make it. My team built it. I just used to come and check and if they were not doing the work, I used to shout at them and ensured they were working till long hours to complete the task. I am also surprised how the bridge fell off"*. The king then asked the elder prince the same question. The prince replied" *I used to come and discuss about the work and daily progress and also if the team was facing any challenges in execution. I also used to help in between if any of my team was struggling with some task. I tried to give them proper rest so that they shall start the next day with full energy and they were also ready to work for me in late hours too"*

The King smiled and made the elder prince the next crown King of the kingdom.

Moral – In business too, one must remember and try winning trust of team through personal power. The position power is always open to use in times of need.

13. Six recruits

In a jungle Mr Bear decided to start a product delivery company. He made a good ware house and then started the work. Soon his business grew and he thought of hiring a team. So, he hired another bear. But that didn't add up much. So, he decided, to increase the team and hire new people. From all the resumes received he selected and hired a monkey, a tortoise, an eagle, a camel and a horse.

Now his business flourished like anything soon. How? Simple. He told the bear to sort the products as per delivery area and be responsible for client servicing. The other five members will be given the products as per their speciality to deliver in the respective areas. If there will be an area which required three or more geographic locations then the products will be delivered in team. In some cases, the eagle will take the product bag and will immediately give to horse if there was a big plain area from where the monkey will take the delivery if there was jungle and swamps.

This use of combination of team and deciding the chart in advance with use of route map and team speciality meant delivery at the scheduled time with less hectic schedule for team and a happy client.

Moral - Operation and services delivery is like a riley race, hence one must choose right team and route and plan accordingly.

14. Akbar and Birbal and Goat

On a beautiful day in spring, the Akbar the Great Emperor, was looking bit disturbed in courtroom. His courtiers were too afraid to ask the sane. After some time, Akbar told his courtiers that he could not sleep last night, because there was some noise coming from back of the palace. He told his one of the courtiers to go and check the issue. The courtier went and came back and told, *"Emperor, last night a goat gave birth to new kids"*. Then Emperor, asked another courtier *"Check out how many kids?"* The courtier went and came back and said *"Emperor, there are four kids"*. Then the emperor again asked," *What is the colour of skin?"* Again, another courtier went and checked and came back saying. *"Emperor, one is black and three are white"*. Emperor again asked *"How many are male and how many females?"* This time again, one of the courtiers when to check. He came back and said *"Emperor, two are male and two are females"*

The Emperor then called for Birbal and told him that he was disturbed last night due to a noise coming from back of the palace and told him to check the issue. Birbal went and came back and replied, *"Emperor, last night a goat gave birth to four kids. Hence there was noise. Out of four kids, two are male and two are females. And one male is of black colour, rest all three kids are of white colour"*.

Moral - In client servicing and even in work try to identify the issue and provide the solution in one go rather than in multiple steps.

15. Salesman and Vacuum Cleaner

Once in afternoon, there was a knock on the door of a flat in a plush building. The lady opened the door and saw a man wearing corporate attire and tie and smiling. He asked for permission to show a product and upon confirmation from the lady, he went into the hall and pulled out a bag full of garbage and with a smiling face inverted that bag's content on the carpet and took out his vacuum cleaner and said in a challenging tone *"Ma'am, if I can't clean the same in ten minutes, then I will eat all the garbage"*. To this the lady replied, *"You will eat it raw or with sauce?"* The salesman had a confused look. The lady replied again *"There is no electricity in house"*

Moral- In sales, please check all the resources before committing.

16. Gold pot vs. Clay Pot

Once there was a King who used to mock his court poet at times because he was not that good looking. The poet was fed up with the comments. One day when king again mocked him, the poet replied very humbly, *"Dear Sir, can I show you something?"* The King nodded in affirmation. The poet then brought two pots filled with water. One was a golden pot decorated with diamonds and pearls. Other was an ordinary clay pot. The poet requested the King to drink water from both pots. The King did so. Then the poet asked *"Dear Sir, can you please tell me, which pot's water was cold?"* The king replied" *Of course, the water of clay pot"*.

Moral – While recruiting a team, check out for the best skills and not the best looks.

17. Top floor in high rise

Once there were four friends who used to work in a city far from home. They used to share a flat and were living their comfortably. The flat was at the sixteenth floor of the building. One day all the friends decided to go for outing to a near by mall. They enjoyed well and were late in night while coming to the residence. They all parked the car in parking and did go to near lift, only to find out that the single lift was not working and was out of order. They had two choice. Either to wait in cold night and see if the lift can be repaired or to climb the stair till sixteenth floor. They choose the second option. They started climbing the floor. First fifth floor they managed happily, next fifth floor they just dragged themselves, next six floor they just pushed themselves due to inner motivation and hard spirit. Upon reaching the gate of the flat, they all were exhausted and were breathing heavily. But suddenly they saw one of the roommates crying bitterly and snatching his hairs. The other three looked upon to him for reason for such behaviour, to this the fourth replied" *I forgot the keys in car*"

Moral – Before going for a herculean task please plan well and check all the resources, rework can be deadly affair.

18. HR manager and Yama

One day while walking down the street a highly successful Human Resources Manager was tragically hit by a bus and she died. Her soul arrived up in heaven where she was met by Yamraj himself. *"Welcome to Heaven,"* said Yamraj. *"Before you get settled in though, it seems we have a problem. You see, strangely enough, we've never once had a Human Resources Manager make it this far and we're not really sure what to do with you."*

"No problem, just let me in," said the woman. *"Well, I'd like to, but I have higher orders. What we're going to do is let you have a day in Hell and a day in Heaven and then you can choose whichever one you want to spend an eternity in." .Actually, I think I've made up my mind, I prefer to stay in Heaven",* said the woman. *"Sorry, we have rules..."* And with that Yamraj put the executive in an elevator and it went down-down-down to hell. The doors opened and she found herself stepping out onto the putting green of a beautiful golf course. In the distance was a country club and standing in front of her were all her friends - fellow executives that she had worked with and they were well dressed in evening owns and cheering for her. They ran up and kissed her on both cheeks and they talked about old times. They played an excellent round of golf and at night went to the country club where she enjoyed an excellent steak and lobster dinner.

She met the Devil who was actually a really nice guy (kind of cute) and she had a great time telling jokes and dancing. She was having such a goodtime that before she knew it, it was time to leave. Everybody shook her hand and waved goodbye as she got on the elevator.

The elevator went up-up-up and opened back up and found Yamraj waiting for her."*Now it's time to spend a day in heaven,*" he said. So, she spent the next 24hours lounging around on clouds and playing the harp and singing. She had great time and before she knew it her 24 hours were up and Yamraj came and got her. "*So, you've spent a day in hell and you've spent a day in heaven. Now you must choose your eternity,*" The woman paused for a second and then replied, "*Well, I never thought I'd say this, I mean, Heaven has been really great and all, but I think I had a better time in Hell.*"

So Yamraj escorted her to the elevator and again she went down-down-down back to Hell.
When the doors of the elevator opened, she found herself standing in a desolate wasteland covered in garbage and filth. She saw her friends were dressed in rags and were picking up the garbage and putting it in sacks. The Devil came up to her and put his arm around her & said "*yesterday we were recruiting you, today you are an employee*"

Moral – In corporate life, don't be lured by plush offices and high spirits. Sometimes a humble place is good to start your job.

19. The real learner

Once in a kingdom there was a gurukul *ashram* which was situated near the bank of a large river. Every day the learned Guru would teach the students about values of life, and also God. The students used to live there and also help Guru in daily chores of the *ashram*. There was a village boy who was very much interested in studies but could not afford *ashram* as his parents were poor and he had to support them for livelihood. So, whenever he used to get time, he used to stand near the gate of the *ashram* and would try to listen to the teachings of the Guru and tried to follow them. The Guru used to see this and used to admire the boy's spirit.

One fine day the Guru told all boys of the *ashram* to go the river and fetch the water in copper vessel for making offering to God. The poor boy also went to fetch the water. When all the students were back, the Guru told all the students to keep the vessels in line. He told the poor boy to keep his vessel also in line. The Guru observed that all vessels were shining from outside and the water inside was bit dirty. When he saw the vessel of the poor boy, the smiled. The vessel was shining from inside and the water was clean. He asked the reason from the boy. The boy *replied "You used to always say that one must have pure heart. Hence I cleaned and washed the vessel from inside".* The Guru praised the boy and he made offering to God from his vessel.

Moral – A good observer always learns right and is praised in terms of recognition and reward.

20. The real successor

Once there was a gurukul in a forest. It was a residential guru-kul. Hence the students used to stay there and learn and also do the daily work of gurukul. The gurukul was famous because of the quality of education and people from all over the kingdom used to study there. The Guru of the ashram was getting old and wanted to look for a worthy successor to run the gurukul. He was in search and finally identified four worthy candidates. After some time, the Guru suddenly felt ill and could not take the classes properly. He called the four candidates and told that he is looking for a successor as he was not keeping well and didn't know how long he will survive. He told that whomsoever will work and make him happy in one month will get the position of successor.

Upon listening to this the students went out in their individual huts and started thinking of how to complete the task. The first student thought that there was always a money problem in gurukul and if he arranges for money then this will make guru happy. So, he went out and started asking for donations from rich families. He himself belonged to a rich family and hence got much sum from his own house. The second student thought of writing a book and giving it to his guru so that he will be happy that he taught his students well. He used to stay in his hut and started writing the book. The third student decided to take care of Guru since he was not keeping well and though that his will make him happy. The fourth student saw that there was chaos in ashram since the guru was not able to take the classes. So, he started taking the classes and also divided the task amongst groups for better administration of the gurukul. Even in holidays of ten days he didn't went to his home though he wanted to see his parents as he had not visited his home for long.

After completion of thirty days the first student entered the guru's hut and offered a bag. When Guru asked, he told *"That gurukul used to face financial crisis at time, hence I have gathered a lot of money to help gurukul run well"*. The guru replied" *It makes me feel good that you were worried for Gurukul"* The second student offered guru a book in velvet cover. Guru opened and read few pages. He smiled and said" *You have learned well from the teachings"*. He then looked upon the third student and praised him saying" *You were very kind to care for me during my illness"*. He didn't saw the fourth student and called for him. When he came bare hand, the guru asked" *Haven't he brought anything?"* The student nodded in negative and asked guru's permission to go as he had to take the evening class and the students were waiting. The guru told that the fourth student will be the successor of the gurukul. He saw the surprise on face of all student. He saw the same and replied" *for me the good and benefit of continuation of ashram is the top most priority and the fourth student has fulfilled the task with utmost satisfaction"*

Moral – Anyone who has his interest aligned with the organisations interest will be the successor in long run.

www.ingramcontent.com/pod-product-compliance
Lightning Source LLC
Chambersburg PA
CBHW030948240526
45463CB00016B/2082